THE LEAN CHANNEL:
YOUTUBE FOR ENTREPRENEURS

By Carey Martell

CEO, Martell Broadcasting Systems, Inc.

MARTELL BOOKS
A division of
Martell Broadcasting Systems, Inc.

Copyright 2015
ISBN: 978-1519247834

First Printing, November 2015

ABOUT THE AUTHOR

Carey Martell is the Chief Executive Officer of Martell Broadcasting Systems, Inc. He is also the founder of the Power Up TV multi-channel network (acquired by Thunder Digital Media in January 2015).

Carey formerly served as the Vice President of Thunder TV, the internet television division of Thunder Digital Media. In the past he has also been the Director of Alumni Membership for Tech Ranch Austin as well as the event organizer for the Austin YouTube Partner monthly meetups. Prior to his role at MBS, Inc. and his career as a video game developer and journalist, Carey served in the US Army for 5 years, including one tour of duty during Operation Iraqi Freedom. Carey is a member of the Veterans of Foreign Wars.

Carey also moonlights as the host of The RPG Fanatic Show, an internet television show which has accumulated over 3.7 million views.

Carey's Personal Blog: http://careymartell.com/

INTRODUCTION

You've heard it before.

A virtually unknown person starts filming videos and once they are uploaded to YouTube, it turns that person into a viral superstar overnight with absolutely no promotion at all. They start making millions of dollars from brand sponsorship deals and their life is forever changed. The videos this person produced were just so exceptionally good that they rose to the top like the proverbial cream in the milk bucket, and the only way that anyone else can repeat that success is to do as they did: just make some videos telling the world who you are and upload them to the internet.

There are forces at work that are desperate to sell us on this fable, but I believe the story is fake. Like so many other stories about success, it is the product of selection bias and after the fact rationalizations.
This book is the result of many years of research, learning iterations and validated feedback to create a scientific approach to the production of web-based video content in order to replicate the successes which new media superstars have often stumbled into.

My philosophies as an entrepreneur hail from my experiences while immersed in the tech startup scene in Austin, Texas. I graduated from an accelerator program run by Tech Ranch Austin, which was founded on boot-strapping lean startup principles. The business framework itself was based on the lean manufacturing processes developed by Toyota to reduce wasted time, money and other resources in their business.

Essentially, lean-based systems are centered on making value-adding components obvious by reducing everything else.

You might be thinking to yourself, "Making a YouTube channel isn't a startup. It's not as ambitious or complicated as something like Facebook or Twitter" but you wouldd be wrong to think that way.

As defined by Eric Ries, author of The Lean Startup, a startup is "a human institution designed to create a new product or service under conditions of extreme uncertainty."

Every film, TV show and yes — YouTube channel -- that has ever been made is a startup. It is only natural to apply lean startup principles to make the process of creating entertainment more efficient.

Most YouTube channels fail to grow an audience. When you analyze the root causes for this failure, a common pattern emerges. The main reason the channels fail is because they don't satisfy audience needs in a way that is better than other alternatives. The lean startup methodology, developed by Eric Ries, tells us that this is a failure of the channel to obtain a "product-market fit."

This means the channel creators did not validate their business model by creating an MVP (minimal viable product) that fits a good market, and for which they can scale the continued manufacturing of a product that satisfies that market.

Your MVP would be the first incarnation of your YouTube channel (perhaps dubbed your Minimum Viable Channel?), which you will constantly improve until you obtain Product/Market Fit. You improve the MVP through cycles of learning —a feedback loop-- that follows the workflow of Build -Measure -Learn.

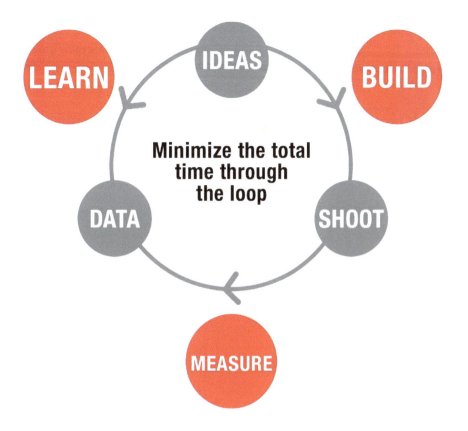

In our context,

"Build" means the goal is to create a video as quickly and cheaply as possible. This is followed by "Measure," where the goal is to determine whether your video is reaching the target audience. Once that determination is reached, you can then reach the "Learn" phase where you decide one of two things:

A)   Persevere by creating a second video with the same format as the first video.
B)   Pivot to change some aspect of your format to better engage the audience that you either want OR discovered accidentally when they liked your first video.

It is important to remember that as a startup, you have no idea who is specifically going to be the audience. You can do research into who your audience might be, but you can only validate your hypothesis during the feedback loop of Build – Measure – Learn. You may often discover that who you thought your audience was for your videos is different than what you originally assumed, which is why this phase is so critical.

How do you find a good market? You do some research. Because YouTube is a search engine, you can do this research very effectively by using tools such as Google AdWords Keyword Planner. This tool locates people who have a problem (such as those looking for specific kinds of videos) and then examines what current videos appear for those search queries in order to gauge how effective the competition is at solving that problem. This often means evaluating the production quality of the video and reviewing the feedback audiences have given on the video comment sections.

There are three stages that all startups share:

1.   **Problem/Solution Fit** (Does this Problem exist? And can I Solve it?)
2.   **Product/Market Fit** (Is my Product desirable? And am I presenting it to the right Market?)
3.   **Scale** (How do I accelerate Growth?)

The first stage is the most important, because all businesses (no matter what they do) exist to solve problems for people who have them. If your business does not solve a problem, it will always fail.

In most startups, you typically measure Problem/Solution Fit by interviews with potential audiences that have the problem; but for a YouTube channel, you can research what kind of videos people are searching for (we'll discuss how to do this later in this course). If you want to experience explosive growth, you often need to find a large (500,000+ people) audience group who has an underserved need, and then make a product that satisfies that need.

You measure the Product/ Market Fit by introducing your MVP into the market and seeing if it is adopted (i.e. watched by people and engaged with). You probably don't think about YouTube videos as a product, but they are. You will not get it right the first time, and it will take many iterations of learning milestones to achieve a perfect Product/Market Fit for your channel.

 The 40% Rule:

How do you measure if you have established product/market fit? Ask your existing audiences if they would become very disappointed if you ceased to continue making videos. If at least 40% of your audience says yes, then you know that you have achieved product/market fit.

Scale in the context of a YouTube channel focused business would be increasing the production of Product (videos) to satisfy your subscriber's demand, while also maximizing the revenue opportunity for the Product by exploring additional revenue streams outside of AdWords such as merchandising, integrated product placements and fan club subscriptions.

This book is divided into four Modules.

> **Module 1** asks you to evaluate yourself as an entrepreneur.
> **Module 2** instructs you in the finer points of story-telling.
> **Module 3** educates you in the basics of bootstrapped video production.
> **Module 4** guides you through the process of introducing your YouTube channel into the market.

Throughout the modules of this book, you will be introduced to many principles that are central to lean startup methodology. The goal is for you to learn them through the creation of the first YouTube videos for a new YouTube channel. In addition to becoming introduced to new ways of thinking about creating videos, you will also inherit various knowledge necessary for the production of audio-visual content. You may already have this knowledge but as this course is written to provide all that is necessary for a YouTuber to begin building their first channel, some advice about the boot-strap production of videos is included.

Thanks for reading. Let the journey begin.

Carey Martell

CEO, Martell Broadcasting Systems, Inc.

August 10th 2015

Introduction **4**

Module I. Your First Channel 10

Section 1. This Is an Adventure **10**
Defining "Success" 10
How to be Successful 11
How David Fights Goliath 11

Section 2. What Do You Want to Achieve? **12**
What Are Your Goals? 12
Who Are You? 14
Putting It All Together 14

Section 3. Who Is Your Audience? **15**
Identifying Your Audience 15
Focus on a Niche, but not a Micro-Niche 20
Additional Channels of Audience Reach 20

Section 4. Choosing a YouTube Channel Name **21**
Customizing Your Channel URL on YouTube 24

Section 5. Deciding Your Brand **24**

Section 6. What Is Your Job as a YouTuber? **26**

Section 7. Your Channel Is a Startup **29**

Section 8. YouTube Terminology **36**
Glossary of YouTube Terminology 36

Module II. Screenwriting **38**

Section 1. Why Write a Screenplay? **38**

Section 2. Elements of a Narrative **39**
Plot 39
Introduction 39
Rising Action 39
Climax 39
Falling Action 39
Resolution 39
Characters 39
Conflict 40
Theme 40

Section 3. Monomyth Narrative Structure **41**
How to Write a Screenplay Using Joseph Campbell's Hero's Journey Model (Monomyth) 41

Section 4. How to Structure a Screenplay **43**
Formatting 44
Screenwriting Software 45

Module III. Video Production **46**
Tips for Operating a Video Camera 46

Section 2. Editing a Video **48**
Exporting Your Video File 50

Section 3. Your Video Intro **50**

Section 4. Your Video Outro (also called an End Slate) **51**
Call to Action End-Slate / Video "Outro" 51
How to Make an End-Slate / Outro 51
Free YouTube End-Slate and Thumbnail .psd Files 51

Section 5. Fair Use and Cover Songs on YouTube **52**
Do I Need a License to do Cover Songs? 52

Section 6. Monetizing Gaming Footage **53**

Section 7. Film Crew Positions Glossary 55

Module IV. Marketing Your YouTube Channel 58

Section 1. YouTube Channel Setup 58

Make Your Channel Look Good 58

Anatomy of a YouTube Channel Front Page 58

YouTube Channel Branded Banner and Avatar 59

YouTube Channel Featured Links 59

Channel Trailer 60

Featured Channels 60

Recent Videos Playlist / Feed 60

Featured Channels Playlist 61

Additional Playlists 61

YouTube Video Thumbnails 61

YouTube Video Description and Tags 61

How to Find Good YouTube SEO Keywords 62

What to Do With the Keywords 64

Try Making Videos Based on Popular Searches 66

Section 2. Setting up Annotations 67

Section 3. Adding a Closed Caption Script 67

Section 4. Understanding the Related Videos Feed 68

Section 5. InVideo Programming, FanFinder 68

YouTube Top Fan G+ Circles 68

InVideo Programming 68

Fan Finder 68

How to Prevent Trolling Attacks on Your YouTube Videos 69

Section 6. Cross-Promotion with Other YouTubers 71

Networking 101 71

Web Rings 71

Where to find collaborators 72

LinkedIn 73

Section 7. Facebook Pages for Beginners 74

Facebook Page Promotion 74

1. Scheduling Posts 74

2. Buying Promoted Posts 75

Facebook Power Editor 76

Section 8. Twitter for Beginners 77

How to Get Video Traffic from StumbleUpon 79

Section 9. Analyzing the Data 81

Other Pointers 83

Section 10. Building a Social Following 84

People 84

Content 85

A Smartly Developed Strategy Is All You Need 86

Last but not Least 87

Final Thoughts 88

Your Journey Begins Now.

MODULE I. YOUR FIRST CHANNEL

Section 1. This Is an Adventure

Congratulations! By starting this course you've taken the first step at becoming a professional YouTuber. Although you may be experienced with the platform and have an existing channel, this course makes the assumption that you are a brand new YouTuber, or that you at least have many questions about how to build an audience for your channel.

With that in mind, this course is designed to guide you step by step on the way to create a video and upload it to your channel for the maximum impact. If you consider yourself to be experienced with YouTube already, I ask that you be patient and please try to read everything without skipping ahead -- you may be surprised to learn there are some basic things you may have neglected to do, and this is why you are having trouble growing an audience.

While YouTube offers a *creator academy course* freely on their website, the course you are taking right now is much more laser-focused on what a YouTuber should be doing to be successful on the platform.

Some of these things are not heavily discussed on the official YouTube course due to conflict with the business model of Google (the parent company of YouTube) and in this course we will discuss those issues while focused 100% on what is most important to YOU: being successful with your channel.

Defining "Success"

Some people have different definitions of success. A lot of YouTubers just see this site as a hobby, and the operate with the idea that getting anyone to watch their videos is a huge success.

In this article, I'm defining "success" in the way that I think most people mean who are putting professional effort into YouTube: building a sustainable small-business producing web videos.

And unless you **really *love* your day job**, that is the same definition you should be using.

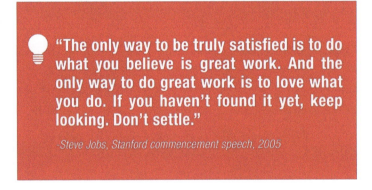

"The only way to be truly satisfied is to do what you believe is great work. And the only way to do great work is to love what you do. If you haven't found it yet, keep looking. Don't settle."

-Steve Jobs, Stanford commencement speech, 2005

Draw a line in the sand today and declare, "I will become a professional YouTuber". It will make things much simpler for you.

How to Be Successful

I previously said that you are starting an adventure. All successful adventures are well planned. Imagine if you were to go camping in the woods; you would want to have a list of things that are very important to your survival, right? Overall, you need water, food, shelter and transportation, but these are broad. "Food" can take numerous forms; anything from donuts to hot dogs can be food.

In the same way, you have some broad things that you need on your YouTube adventure to be successful, but each of these items can be broken down into very specific things.

Broadly, you need:

1.   Screenwriting
2.   Video Production
3.   Video Editing
4.   Marketing

But each of these things need to be broken down much further so that you can incorporate them into your strategy.

In this course we will go over each topic and how to do it at the most basic level of operation.

While taking this course, I ask that you keep something in mind: no matter how small you start, you can build a large channel. Many people have done it, and you can do it too.

How David Fights Goliath

The essential strategic insight for small YouTube channels competing for views against larger channels is simply this:

Find Ways to Compete Other Than on Big Budget Production Values

In the competition for best quality information, or personal engagement with your viewers, or knowledge about the topic you are discussing, you are quite possibly able to offer something that the larger YouTube channels cannot match.

Smaller channels can compete against the larger channels dominating search results, but you have to be creative about it. For small channels the key advantage is the creation of a personal atmosphere; a community around your video content.

Viewers also truly enjoy being able to comment back and forth with the owner of the channel, which is hard for larger channels to do when hundreds of people comment every day.

To be successful you must be viewer focused:

Give People What They Want

You can't compete on production values with the larger channels, because they have more money to dump into their videos. Refuse to compete that way. Instead, make something so original that people will come back to your channel just to see what's new. The big channels are predictable. They have found a format that works and they keep repeating the same formula. But there is a large market that wants something else, and you can win them over by being unpredictable and surprising them.

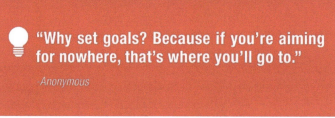

"Why set goals? Because if you're aiming for nowhere, that's where you'll go to."
-Anonymous

Section 2. What Do You Want to Achieve?

Before we get into laser-focused detail about what you need to be successful, we first need to learn some information about you. This will tailor the kind of show that you produce so that it perfectly suits you.

The first training you need is for your mind and spirit. Again, you are embarking on an adventure. You will be tried and tested. It will not be an easy path. Even when you find success, you may discover a thousand screaming teenage girls chasing you around VidCon.

If you stand for nothing, you'll fall for anything. Let's figure out what you stand for.

What Are Your Goals?

Let's go old-school. Find some paper and a pen.

Something that highly successful people do is focus. We don't flip-flop around the world wondering what the next step is; we know what it is, because we have clearly-defined goals to accomplish in life. As long as we keep our gaze focused on these goals, although we may wander, we are never lost.

Bruce Lee is an example of a highly successful person. Before he became the most famous martial arts super-star in the world, he was an actor struggling to make it. He had just been fired from The Green Hornet, and passed over for Kung-Fu in favor of David Carradine.

Then one day in 1969, Bruce Lee wrote the following mission statement for himself:

My Definite Chief Aim

I, Bruce Lee, will be the first highest paid Oriental super Star in the United States. In return I will give the most exciting performances and render the best of quality in the capacity of an actor. Starting 1970 I will achieve world fame and from then onward till the end of 1980 I will have in my possession $10,000,000. I will live the way I please and achieve inner harmony and happiness.

Bruce Lee
Jan. 1969

Transcript

SECRET

My Definite Chief Aim

I, Bruce Lee, will be the first highest paid Oriental super star in the United States. In return I will give the most exciting performances and render the best of quality in the capacity of an actor. Starting 1970 I will achieve world fame and from then onward till the end of 1980 I will have in my possession $10,000,000. I will live the way I please and achieve inner harmony and happiness.

Bruce Lee
Jan. 1969

That year Bruce Lee starred in several more TV shows, and in 1971 he co-wrote and starred in the lead role of The Big Boss. He became the most famous actor in Hong Kong, and the rest is history.

If Bruce Lee can do it, so you can you.

Here is your first assignment:

- Write down a list of five things that you want to achieve with your channel.

These are your goals. This is what we're going to work toward while creating your channel. Your channel exists to allow you to achieve these things.

Hold on to this list, because we are going to use it later.

Who Are You?

Let's back up for a moment.

Do you *really* have an honest, accurate assessment of yourself and your abilities?

Many creators have doomed themselves by over-estimating exactly what they are good at.

As a YouTuber, your job ultimately is to be an entertainer. You can be other things in addition (such as a game reviewer, a teacher, a prankster) but to be successful in front of a camera *requires* the ability to entertain. John Stewart, host of The Daily Show, is both a comedian and a journalist. He knows that he is an entertainer and he embraces it. So should you.

When I first got into the business, my assessment of myself wasn't 100% accurate. I spent years trying to be successful without fully understanding myself. Then two years ago I enrolled in a startup accelerator course for my YouTube network. My mentor required me to take a personality test and use that information to focus on my core strengths.

Today I run a YouTube network that gained over 1,000 Partners in six months, and I use the lessons from that course every day.

So let's learn some things about you and build from there.

I recommend that you take a Myers Briggs Type Indicator personality test to learn more about yourself. You can do paid tests, but there are also free quizzes online that will give you a rough assessment, such as this test from *http://www.teamtechnology.co.uk/mmdi/questionnaire/*

Another book that I like to use in conjunction with Myers Briggs Type Indicator is Strengths Finder. You can order it off of Amazon.

Doing these tests are optional, but I promise that the insight you'll gain about yourself will change the way you interact with others, both on and off-screen.

When I took these tests I learned that I am a Myers-Briggs **INFJ Type Indicator** and my Strengths Finder themes were **Strategic, Achiever, Command, Ideation and Individualization.**

This taught me that I was a natural leader, but an important part of my leadership is my ability to mentor and teach other people. You might say the reason this exam exists is because I listened to the things these tests told me about myself.

This is why I'm a big believer in first understanding who you are before you set about trying to succeed in life. If it works for me, it can work for you.

Putting It All Together

Okay, so if you have followed all of my advice so far, you now have a much clearer understanding of who you are and what you want out of your channel. It's time to write your own mission statement.

Go ahead and write it down on your notepad. Keep it. Laminate it if you must. Just never forget it. It might end up in a museum someday.

(If you haven't taken the personality tests yet, that's okay. Just fill in what you can and progress to the next module. You can always come back to this section later and do the tests)

Quiz Questions: Who Are You?

1. What is your Briggs-Myers Personality Type? (if you took the test)
2. What are your Strengths-Finder themes? (if you took the test)
3. What are the five things you want to achieve with your channel?
4. Based on your personality type and Strengths Finder themes, how do you think you can best achieve your goals?
5. Taking all of the above into consideration, what will your YouTube channel be about?

Section 3. Who Is Your audience?

"Now that we know who you are, I know who I am." - Elijah Price, Unbreakable (2000)

Ultimately your success on YouTube depends on your ability to appeal to other folks who will enjoy your videos. Satisfying your audience is vastly more important than any other factor in the creative process, and at times you may need to sacrifice your personal vision in order to appease your fan base.

This is the reality of being an entertainer.

Before you produce videos, you should figure out who your audience is and what they want to see. We must perform "market research" before we actually produce a video.

Identifying Your Audience

You must be very laser-focused on who you want your videos to appeal to. It is tough to appeal to everyone. Game review channels are one of the most popular types of shows on YouTube, but every popular channel is designed to appeal to very specific niches within the gaming community. Let's analyze a few popular channels and see what these differences are.

Angry Joe Show *http://www.youtube.com/user/AngryJoeShow*

• Joe focuses almost exclusively on reviews and previews of current-gen games. He also does news reports and top 10 lists.

• Appearance wise, Joe is the GQ Magazine version of a nerd. He looks crisp and trendy, and he is always wearing that black Superman shirt (the one he wore during the Return of Superman series) and leather jacket. He's cool, and he sports the ideal image of what many gamers would like to be.

• Joe's background is animated; his show has a lot of chroma-key involved, so it's a professionally produced work. Joe also tends to have good but gentle music in his backgrounds while he's talking.

• When Joe does cut-aways, he uses a lot of slow motion zooms on images or footage to keep the audience interested.

• Joe's rants are angry but they are backed by research. He also discusses gaming issues that have international importance, giving him an international appeal. His assessments also consider transmedia; he talks about the business of games and the ecosystem of the entertainment industry quite frequently. He is a resource for gamers to receive high quality news.

• Joe focuses on using comedy to get his point across, which makes it easier for the audience to stay interested in what he's talking about. He has the Daily Show effect working in his favor.

• Joe often incorporates other trusted news sources into his videos, giving his opinions a sense of legitimacy through association with the professionally produced interviews or trailers he is commenting on.

• Joe's onscreen persona is that of a "champion of the people" for gamers, focused on old-school appreciations and values. The reason he focuses so much hate on DLC packs is because it's a new business model that the majority of his audience is hesitant to embrace.

• Joe often talks about a problem in a title and then offers a solution, if he can think of one.

• Joe also shows an occasional vulnerable side, like when he asks the audience for help or admits that he honestly doesn't have an answer to a question. This makes him a more relatable character.

JonTron Show *http://www.youtube.com/user/JonTronShow*

• Jon is like Mystery Science Theatre 3000 for retro gamers. He often invents internal voices for characters in the games he plays, and makes tons of pop culture references. Sometimes he even has conversations with the characters. His videos exist in this surreal world that kinda-almost takes place in reality (a lot of gaming shows have this alternate reality feel to them).

- Jon uses a lot of fast zooms in his edits to create humorous effects.

- The games Jon plays are really just an accessory; people are watching because Jon is entertaining, not because the games are. Playing videogames is just a theme.

- Jon sometimes breaks out into humorous songs.

- His videos are structured to be a collage of different media (video, audio, music and sounds) to support the opinions that he forms about the games.

- Jon often does fan requests, and solicits them in his videos.

Gaming Historian *http://www.youtube.com/user/mcfrosticles*
- Gaming Historian uses a lot of slow zooms on pictures, coupled with fades to black or white. His show relies heavily on stock photos and footage, although there are some custom images created to help support his arguments.

- He does well researched articles of edutainment; he uses a lot of quotes to support his arguments, and the humor (if at all) is pretty dry. There are also a lot of narrative embellishments to create drama in the story, with statements like "rushed in...charged ahead..." and such to describe business decisions.

- Much of the music playing in the background is from classic video games, which adds an element of nostalgia to the videos.

Guru Larry *http://www.youtube.com/larry*
- Larry is a hypothetical example as if one of the smart-ass cynical characters in a Monty Python skit decided to start reviewing video games.

- Larry specializes in retro games that were developed and released for the UK. He does review games that were released in North America, but he focuses on the PAL version of those titles. He also occasionally reviews movies.

- Larry often uses limited animation techniques on a cartoon caricature of himself, especially his collaboration videos. His videos sport a lot of motion graphics in the editing.

- Many of the games Larry talks about are really crappy, so he is able to make fun of the games. And because there aren't many people reviewing PAL-only games from people's childhoods, he is able to monopolize the YouTube search pages for those titles.

- Like JonTron and Angry Joe, Larry does a lot of top ten lists.

- Outside of his show, Larry heavily engages with other gamers using Skype and Facebook groups.

Gamester81 *http://www.youtube.com/user/Gamester81*
- Gamester81 is that rich dude in your neighborhood who is always coming over after work to show off his latest thing-a-ma-bob. His videos primarily focus on game systems that weren't well known or that failed in the market, or additional peripherals.

- Gamester81 has a consistent look; he always wears a baseball cap in reverse.

- A lot of the items in his collection are hard to find, or are outright rare. His videos are one of the few ways gamers have to get close to an actual working unit.

- In the early days, he was one of the most subscribed gaming channels on YouTube. This was primarily because of his massive game collection.

- Gamester81 has a gentle way of talking. He's like your favorite geek uncle.

- His newest videos have more use of motion graphics and chroma key.

- He has done a large number of collaboration videos, sometimes doing tours at other gamers' houses to look at their collections.

- He started a website with dozens of other gaming channels signed up as contributors. He's known for being a very approachable and social person in the retro game collecting scene.

The Game Chasers *http://www.youtube.com/user/Captain8Bit*
- Billy and Jay are American Pickers for retro game collectors. The show is absolutely 100% edited the exact same way and they have the same co-hosts dynamic -- and it works.

• Unlike in American Pickers, Billy and Jay are competing to build their own personal collections. They race to find a good game before the other does, but there is still this level of respect between them which many game collectors can identify with.

• Many gamers who don't have the disposable income to build a massive game collection watch the show to live vicariously through them, but many die-hard collectors also watch for tips and tricks to help them in their own hunts.

• Each episode is an adventure where they might find a super rare game worth hundreds or thousands of dollars. There is some actual tension in the videos due to this factor, and it makes it very engaging to watch.

• They sometimes do animated specials that bring in many of the notable game channels they collaborate with, usually done in the style of an Aqua Teen Hunger Force episode.

The Angry Video Game Nerd *http://www.youtube.com/user/JamesNintendoNerd*
• The prototypical YouTube video game show, AVGN invented the genre. Because he is the progenitor, elements of his show format are common in almost all game review web series (such as JonTron). This is especially true about his show existing in a surreal universe where he can interact with the characters in the games the same way that a child might talk to bad guys on the TV screen, only the adventure on the TV screen typically spills out into the AVGN's game room. The AVGN universe is probably best called "childhood nostalgia," and he is the host guiding you through that universe.

• One of AVGN's strongest selling points is that he "takes people back to the past". This line is even in his theme song. The song is telling you exactly what he's going to do and what the premise of the show is; re-living nostalgia and reminiscing about "better days", which for many guys in their 30s and 40s, that was playing games that are quite awful (by today's standards).

• Like Angry Joe, AVGN has a uniform he wears in every episode: the stereotypical white shirt, glasses and pocket protector attire for a 1980s film nerd.

• There are often sub-stories within the episodes. A good example is the *Christmas Wish* list videos. The larger narrative is the 80's time period, the smaller narrative is the contents of the Sears Shopping catalogs. The even smaller narrative is the mini-reviews of games and items that appeared inside that catalog.

• AVGN puts a lot of effort into the editing of the videos. His opening is long and has a theme song, but he also edits a brand new collage of game footage and show clips for every episode's title sequence (Which is the only reason people don't just skip through it. Normally an opening shouldn't be longer than 10-20 seconds). You can tell that he is a perfectionist who cares deeply about ensuring that his audience is engaged by the way he edits the video. He frequently talks directly to the audience the way that he would talk to a friend sitting on his couch, which makes you feel like you **ARE** sitting on the couch with him.

The notable thing about shows like AVGN is that the videos are legitimately entertaining. The point of his videos isn't to educate you about games. They do that, but only because the vehicle in which he is working requires him to talk about the games.

In particular, the AVGN videos are actually a comedy -- a parody on game reviews and those stereotypical angry players who break their controllers and start flame-wars on internet forums. AVGN episodes have re-watchability because it's about the character and the mad world that he lives in. A video focused 100% on a game review has poor re-watchability.

Focus on a Niche, but not a Micro-Niche

To make decent money from YouTube AdWords, you need to be able to acquire hundreds of thousands of views per video. This means that you need at least 100,000 people interested in watching your show on a regular basis.

If you make beauty videos, you have to be sure that many people will be interested in the products and makeup lessons that you want to demonstrate. It will not do you any good to invest time, energy and money into making a video that will only be of interest to a few hundred people.

To research audiences, use the *Google Keyword Planner* to see how many unique monthly searches are conducted for different types of topics. Try to find search phrases that are getting 100,000 + per month, and that do not have very good videos on the first page of YouTube's search results. This will make it easier to get noticed.

You can also perform a trick on the YouTube search field itself. Simply type in the keyword phrase of something that your video is about, and the drop-down menu will recommend highly searched phrases related. These are all things being searched for often, and by sticking these keywords into your video title and description, your video will rank better in the search results and appear to those who conduct those searches.

Additional Channels of Audience Reach

You can no longer rely entirely on video search engine optimization techniques. YouTube has hundreds of hours of videos uploaded to the site every minute. You will need to get your videos featured on other websites if you want to reach the audience who would like to watch them.

Your first step is to identify which blogs would feature your videos. To do this, type the search phrases you found from the Google and YouTube keyword tools into *Google Blog Search.*

For example, if you are making an original web series that is science-fiction based, you would want to search for science fiction related blogs and ask the owners to feature your videos. There is almost always a Contact page on a website, and you can email the site owners asking for your video to be featured. Bloggers often struggle to produce enough content to keep their readers interested, and they might be interested in cross-promotion with you. They can share your videos and you will do interviews for them. This will bring your channel's audience to their website when you share that interview to your fans on Twitter and Facebook.

You can also look for Facebook groups focused on your videos area of expertise, like pranks, cooking, gaming, etc. Sub-Reddits can also be very effective, too.

Basically, any website off-YouTube that has a community of people interested in the same subject matter as your videos are potential places to find an audience for your channel. Don't just upload videos to YouTube and expect miracles; if you are not promoting your video, then you shouldn't expect others to.

But keep one thing in mind...

We're not marketing your videos just yet.

All this research is to help you figure out **what videos to make** and **how you are going to get people to watch them.**

Essentially, we are identifying what the Problem/Solution Fit for your channel is.

I like to take a bottom-up approach from things; most people would make a video they think would be fun and then try to figure out how to get others to watch it. That's not the best approach.

It is better to first figure out what ***OTHER*** people would be interested in watching and then produce that video.

Like I said earlier, your job is to be an entertainer. Your job isn't to amuse yourself.

It's quiz time. I assume you have done the research that I told you to do?

Quiz Questions: Who Is Your Audience?

1. What will your first video be about?

2. I have researched the audience for this video. (True / False)

3. What keyword phrases did you find to help this video get discovered on YouTube?

4. What blogs did you find that might feature your video when it's done?

5. Are there any other places you can think of where you might be able to find audiences for your video?

Section 4. Choosing a YouTube Channel Name

Choosing a YouTube Channel Name

When creating a new account, you may be confused about how to customize your channel username. At the bottom of this module is a video that will show you step by step how to set it up, but first let's talk about deciding your channel name.

A lot of people choose usernames for personal reasons, and that is fine; but if you want to build a business with your YouTube channel, you should consider choosing a name that is going to help you in search engine results.

My original Partner channel was *'jfreedan'.* I eventually realized that this is not a great keyword, so I moved my gaming content over to an account named *TheRPGFanatic* (because the name of my show on jfreedan was 'The RPG Fanatic').

One of the videos on my old channel is about cosplay, so let's use the term "cosplay" as a base to discuss the process to choose YouTube channel user names.

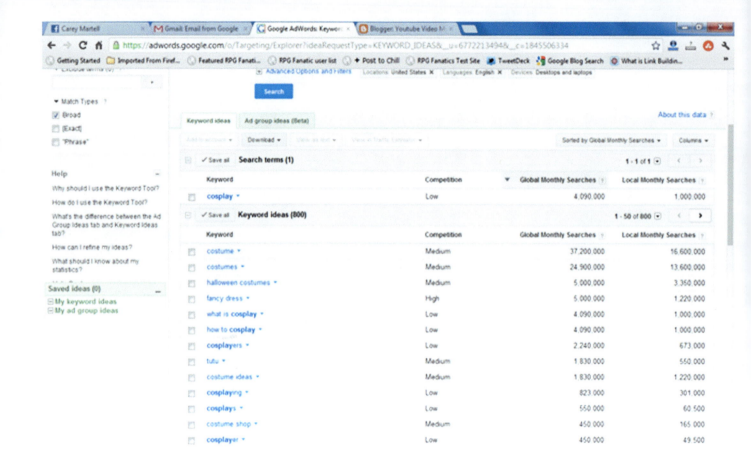

By using the **AdWords keyword tool** I can see that "cosplay" receives 4 million global searches every month on Google Search, with 1 million of these searches performed by users who are local to my geographical area.

I can also see related keywords, such as "costume". That keyword receives 37 million global searches, with 16 million of them from users local to me.

Additionally, "What is cosplay" and "how to cosplay" receive 4 million global searches. These are all keywords I should be incorporating into my YouTube video descriptions and channel description area.

Unfortunately the username that would be most ideal for my show, "HowtoCosplay" already exists; http://www.youtube.com/howtocosplay

It is also under-utilized, but I notice that the channel does have a video on it that has over 100,000 views. My first instinct is to reach out to the owner of the channel and ask to purchase the channel. This would actually save me some trouble because the channel already has some presence and lots of activity.

But is the channel even for sale and if so, at a price I can afford? Probably not.

The channel http://www.youtube.com/user/cosplaytutorials also exists, but has been abandoned for over a year. The chances of being able to purchase this channel are rather low because the owner has not logged into the account since August 2011.

On the other hand, http://www.youtube.com/user/whatiscosplay does not exist, so the channel name is available.

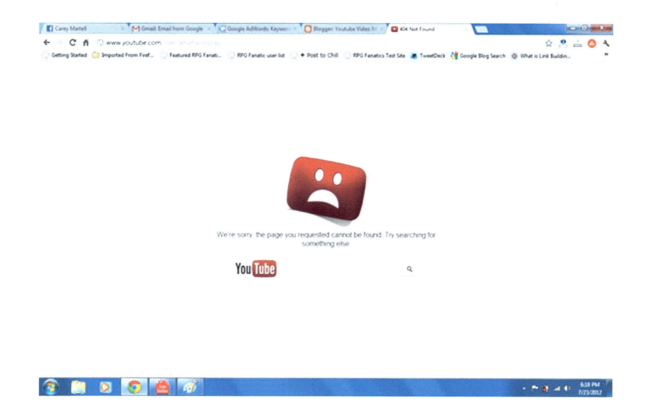

When you see a screen like this, it means the channel username doesn't exist and you can make it.

So to make a channel about cosplaying, I will create a YouTube channel with that username. This is because even though it isn't the most ideal channel name, the keyword "what is cosplay" still receives 4 million global searches per month on Google.

The next step is to optimize the channel for appearing in search engine results related to the keyword "cosplay". For this we edit the channel info.

I will post the text here so you can see what I wrote and why,

*"On this channel you can learn **how to cosplay** and receive **costume ideas.** We will teach you how to make lots of amazing **anime costumes!** You will also be able to purchase items from our **costume shop!** Happy **cosplaying**!"*

Every underlined phrase is a keyword that was recommended by the Google AdWords keyword tool.

The tags for the channel are also selected from the recommendations of the tool.

This is the process I use to create channel names for YouTube, and I recommend that you do the same thing. Having a username that has keywords many people are searching for will make it easier to improve SEO (search engine optimization) for your channel later, which is vital in order to get any traffic to your videos within YouTube.

When I decide what videos to make, I use this same process: I look at the subjects related to the topic of my channel that people are searching for on YouTube and Google, and then I make a video that fits the most popular search phrases.

Customizing Your Channel URL on YouTube

It used to be very easy to choose your channel URL but since 2013, YouTube has made it more difficult to do so. This video tutorial will show you how to change your channel URL from a string of gibberish numbers and letters, into a custom username.

Quiz Questions: Your YouTube Channel Username

1. It is okay for my channel username to be the generic string of random numbers and letters YouTube generates when I first make my account. (True / False)

2. I should pick an original YouTube channel username that is easy for people to remember and describes the type of videos my channel will have. (True / False)

3. Creating a YouTube username is a lot like picking a website domain name. I should use search engine optimization to help choose. (True / False)

4. "CoolGuy1985" is a good channel name to have. (True / False)

5. Before picking my channel name, I should research what types of keyword phrases people search for online, and create a name that utilizes those keywords. (True / False)

Section 5. Deciding Your Brand

How to Create a Super Brand for Your YouTube Channel

Your YouTube channel is ultimately a brand. There are hundreds of channels on the market for every content niche; they are essentially offering the same types of entertainment as other channels in their niche. What generally sets them apart is the brand image of the channel.

A brand is more than your product, your marketing image or your business numbers. It is the way people see and remember your company.

A brand is about the reactions you get from people (especially customers) when they see your commercial, an image with your products or maybe your logo placed on top of a building. The brand image is how you communicate with people, and how they perceive your business as a whole.

A super brand will take this level of communication to the highest peaks. If you want to get your brand up to this level then you should reflect on these:

- **Loyalty at customer level:** This means that whenever your product is compared to a competitor's product, the customer will always pick yours, in spite of the fact that the customer has other choices. Super brands always find an effective way to convince customers that their products are the best, so it is worth buying them.

- **Taking over the market:** With high quality products and great services, a super brand will always manage to win customers over, winning a bigger market share than competitors.

- **Built to last:** Through intense and thorough market studies, constant improvements and leading innovation, a super brand will never get satisfied to sit in the shadows. It will always look to improve its products to help ensure a longer stay on the market and in the preferences of people worldwide.

- **Generate value:** Your marketing statements must be accompanied by great products in order develop the brand to a high level of recognition.

- **High acceptance of the market:** This means that your product or service will always cover the market demand, no matter how high. A super brand will always be prepared to face any increase in demand, and to make sure that the products are always available.

Building a super brand is not the easiest thing, but with a sustained marketing campaign and continual delivery of value to your channels, anyone can end up at the top of the pyramid.

To ensure that your brand will start making this climb, make sure that the products and services that you deliver will always be satisfying your Partners. Keeping them satisfied will ensure both success and longevity on the market. You also must always be looking for further improvements. For this you must research what competitors are doing to see exactly what customers expect from you and how you can improve what you deliver to them. Also, observe how your competition stands up, and analyze what you can do better in order to attract their customers over to your side.

Power Up TV
Sponsored

Power up your YouTube views by joining www.powerup.tv ,one of the fastest growing MCN for geeks and gamers! Get a FREE copy of Xsplit Broadcaster when you join! Up to 95% ad revenue split, no lock-in contracts. Huge free music library to use in your videos. Get free games. BONUS: Recruit channels and you'll get PAID 15% of their ad revenue!

Like Comment Share

This Facebook ad for Power Up TV has consistent branding, and clearly communicates the value proposition of joining the network.

To develop your brand image for your network, you should follow the Three Rules of Marketing:

Positioning: Identify and attempt to occupy a market niche for a brand, product or service, while utilizing traditional marketing placement strategies (i.e. price, promotion, distribution, packaging, and competition).

Advertising: Build awareness of the product by making the brand message highly visible. This can be paid advertising, but it can also be something as simple as a website that ranks highly on search engines.

Your network's brand should have a color, a logo and a slogan. Using the super brand you can then design the products and campaigns that have a consistent imagery with super brand. Everything from video thumbnails, to blog posts, to featured images should conform to the standards that you set. A great example of this consistency can be seen in the Power Up TV website itself.

Deliver value: Provide the customer with what was promised.

If you truly want to understand marketing, then you should study the propaganda of Vladimir Lenin. The goal of Lenin was to convince the Russian people to dramatically change their culture and behavior; it was very effective. To achieve this, he hired the best designers and copy-editors in his day to design posters and produce films. Even educational material like pamphlets and books were designed to convince the Russian people to change their behaviors.

When you get down to it, that is what marketing is: convincing people to take a specific action you want them to take. In the case of Power Up TV, we want people to join our YouTube network. Your objective should be to convince audiences to watch your videos and become a subscriber to your channel.

You should also remember the other important lesson in marketing: **Deliver.**

The Soviet Union had fantastic marketing, but unfortunately it also had a really crappy product: communism.

The Soviet Union failed to deliver on its promises to the Russian people, which is why eventually it was overthrown.

You don't want to be over-thrown. Deliver on your promises to your audience, and you will be able to retain them.

Section 6. What Is Your Job as a YouTuber?

Let me level with you for a moment. What I'm going to say is the most important thing for **ALL** YouTubers to hear.

Making videos is NOT your job.

If you want to make money producing videos, go onto eLance and offer your services to produce commercials for other people. Commercial work is the only way to make money producing videos.

The business of YouTube is NOT producing videos. **It's advertising.**

There are many folks who have reached out to me to work as a consultant for them, but when I tell them that they need to focus more on advertising, marketing, and sponsorships -- the stuff that makes all the money for your channel -- they tell me things like "I don't want to sell out" or "my audience will get turned off."

All they really want to do is screw around with their camera, produce an original screenplay that they wrote, or get someone to watch their *let's play* videos.

If you think like that, I am going to be blunt:

If you are worried about audiences hating you because you're a "Sell Out", you are not a professional.

If you think like that, you are a hobbyist who is trying to make videos because you are compensating for inadequacies in your life. You want to be loved and appreciated more than you want to build a business.

If that is the case, I can't help you.

Your job as a YouTuber is to produce videos that will be suitable for brands to advertise their products and services on. You build an audience so you can market to them.

This is the business of radio and television, and it is the business of web video, too. Advertising has been the business of TV since the first TV show aired.

This is the reality of the web video market. If you put your show behind a pay-wall, and in that 1 in a million chance that your videos do become popular, someone else will just download your videos, and throw them on Bittorrent "as a fan for other fans". You will go broke because as a creator with no industry relations to leverage for your content, you don't have things like theatrical ticket sales and premium advertiser upfronts like major film and TV studios do.

I can show you the path to success, but you must be willing to walk down it yourself.

If you follow my advice in this course, you will build an audience and you will make money with your channel. If you don't follow my advice, you might build an audience but you will not make much money. This will largely be due to the fact that you built an unmonetizable audience who won't respond to integrated advertising, and who will use ad-blocking software every time they watch your videos.

What Is an Unmonetizable Audience?

Let's take reddit as an example.

reddit is one of the most popular websites on the internet, but it's one of the least profitable. The site actually loses money every day, but is kept afloat with investor money.

The problem is that reddit's founders valued building a huge audience over building a sustainable business. They implemented policies like "no self-promotion," and having an army of volunteer mods do the bulk of the community building work. How to make money was an after-thought, and this is a problem because reddit requires a team of developers to maintain it, and the bandwidth costs are very expensive.

Because reddit cultivated a community of people who hate advertising, reddit has not been able to deliver good results for companies who buy ads on the platform. Advertisers end up getting anonymous trolls -- some of whom may be hired by competitors -- to downvote and post misleading comments on the paid ads. This turns off most advertisers because they don't want to pay for bad service. They expect to buy an ad for, say $500, and get back $1,250 in sales. reddit cannot deliver on this, and so the site is financially unstable. This may actually lead to it shutting down in the next few years when investors finally stop giving them money and hoping reddit can be sold to someone else for a big pay day.

You need to understand that "being loved" is not your job as a YouTuber. Your job is to build an audience that will respond to advertisers, so that you can re-invest into making more videos, pay your own bills, buy food, send your kids to college someday, etc. If you want this to be your career, then you need to treat it like a business. The love of your customers is a byproduct of a successful business model, and it should never be the primary goal.

Some of the most popular YouTubers do not actually make a lot of money on YouTube itself. Instead, their day job is to produce commercials for other companies and then plug those commercials into Twitter, Facebook and their e-mailing lists. The most successful YouTubers pre-sell sponsored ads in all their videos for tens of thousands of dollars per video.

You absolutely need audiences to love your videos, and possibly even you. Oprah and Stephen Colbert are examples of hosts who command large, intensely passionate audiences that deeply love them, but they are also monetized audiences. Both Oprah and Colbert frequently promote books on their shows, which results in those books selling so many copies that they become best-sellers. You are pretty much guaranteed to become a best-selling author if either of these celebrities mentions your book to their audiences. That's powerful, and it means publishers are willing to spend a lot of money to get the books on the shows, because the audiences are valuable.

So I stress again, the only audience that matters to your success are the folks like this.

They are the segment of your audience who enables you to make a living doing your show. From day on, you should make sure that you are engaging with this segment as much as you can, and producing a show that they want to watch.

You need to grow an audience who is not only okay with ads, but who might actually share those ads with other people. Does that sound weird? Remember, music and game trailers are ads; some of the most popular content on YouTube are ads.

It is a misconception that people hate ads. The truth is, certain types of people don't like certain types of ads. Many people like ads for products that they are interested in, which is why the operation of the entire YouTube website is successfully funded solely by ads.

To avoid making the same mistake as reddit, while producing your videos do not do things like criticize other YouTubers for having advertiser sponsorship deals. Also do not make statements about how you hate certain types of companies that may someday want to advertise on your channel. If you do things like this, you will build an audience that will turn on you when you do start trying to monetize through sponsorships.

The people who make the most money on YouTube are gamers and beauty gurus. This is because they build audiences interested in the consumer products featured in the videos. There are other niches which can be profitable too, and you can make money doing an original web series if you focus on integrated brand sponsorships (i.e. featuring brand name clothing and food in your show so the audience can read the labels). There are also merchandising opportunities for you, beyond the stereotypical t-shirts and hats..

There are many great examples of merchandising in TV shows and films. One of my favorite examples is the TalkBoy from Home Alone 2. This was originally just a non-working prop in the film, but based on an overwhelming interest from kids who watched the movie in theaters, Tiger Electronics bought the license from the film-makers. They then created a real TalkBoy and launched the product in time for the VHS home release of Home Alone 2. It was one of the best selling toys that year.

Once you understand this truth about your job as a YouTuber, you have the power to stop your unproductive habits.

• You won't make videos haphazardly about whatever comes to mind.

• You won't launch Kickstarters for films and web series that appeal only to you and your small circle of closest film-making friends.

- You won't max out your credit cards by making a romantic comedy web series -- or, god forbid, a drama -- that will be incredibly difficult to market because the audiences for those niches are not readily available on YouTube.

- You won't attract an audience of people who hate advertising and will use ad blocking software when watching your videos, or who will troll you when you do product endorsements in your videos.

What you will do is follow the productive habits outlined in this course and find success.

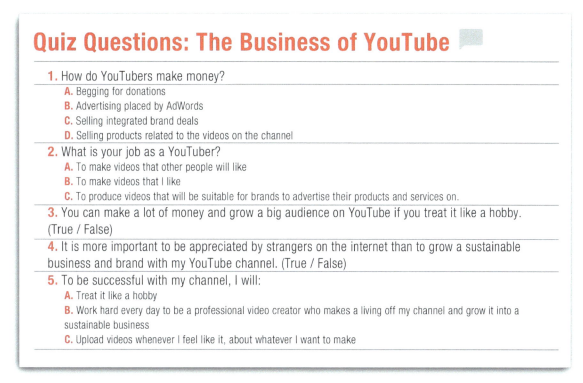

Quiz Questions: The Business of YouTube

1. How do YouTubers make money?
   A. Begging for donations
   B. Advertising placed by AdWords
   C. Selling integrated brand deals
   D. Selling products related to the videos on the channel

2. What is your job as a YouTuber?
   A. To make videos that other people will like
   B. To make videos that I like
   C. To produce videos that will be suitable for brands to advertise their products and services on.

3. You can make a lot of money and grow a big audience on YouTube if you treat it like a hobby. (True / False)

4. It is more important to be appreciated by strangers on the internet than to grow a sustainable business and brand with my YouTube channel. (True / False)

5. To be successful with my channel, I will:
   A. Treat it like a hobby
   B. Work hard every day to be a professional video creator who makes a living off my channel and grow it into a sustainable business
   C. Upload videos whenever I feel like it, about whatever I want to make

Section 7. Your Channel Is a Startup

If you want to be a professional YouTuber (someone who earns enough revenue from videos to make it a full-

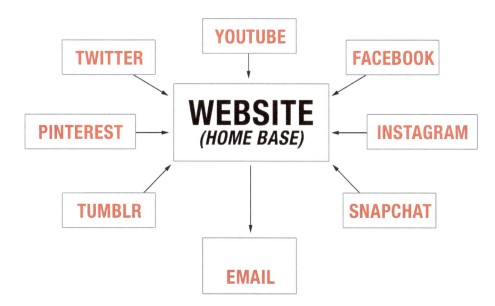

time career) then you need to think about your YouTube channel as more than just a profile to upload videos to. You need to think of the operation of your channel as a business, and build a business plan around your channel.

Therefore, your YouTube channel is a startup company. By keeping this in mind it will be easier for you to make decisions about it.

Lean startup canvas is a template for your business plan. I have modified it for the development of a YouTube channel.

Lean Canvas   Project Name   01-Jan-2014 / Iteration #x

Problem	Solution	Unique Value Proposition	Unfair Advantage	Customer Segments
Top 2-3 problems	Top 3 features	Single, clear, compelling message that states why you are different and worth paying attention	Can't be easily copied or bought	Target customers
	Key Metrics Key activities you measure		**Channels** Path to customers	

Cost Structure	Revenue Streams
Customer Acquisition costs Distribution costs Hosting People, etc.	Revenue Model Life Time Value Revenue Gross Margin

PRODUCT   MARKET

To help you better understand how to use this sheet, here is an example of the canvas applied to my personal YouTube channel.

Lean Canvas   The RPG Fanatic   01-Jan-2014 / Iteration #x

Problem	Solution	Unique Value Proposition	Unfair Advantage	Customer Segments
Top 2-3 problems	*Top 3 features*	*Single, clear, compelling message that states why you are different and worth paying attention*	*Can't be easily copied or bought*	*Target audiences*
1. Top YouTube game reviewers are not hardcore RPG fans and often don't give reviews valuable to the core customer.	Develop a game review show from the perspective of a hardcore RPG Fan.	Fanatical reviews and commentary about roleplaying videogames from a true fan of the genre.	Host is genuinely passionate & knowledgeable about niche interest RPGs (expertise)	1. Fans of retro RPG games 2. Fans of niche publisher RPG games (NIS America, Gust Co. Nihon Falcon, etc.)
2. People search YouTube for reviews about niche interest RPGs and find low-quality videos.	**Key Metrics** *Key activities you measure* 1. YouTube Views 2. Comments 3. Subscribers		**Channels** *Path to customers* • Special interest forums (rpgs) • Facebook Groups • Organic search results. • Collab videos	*Target brands* 1. Publishers of niche RPGs 2. Specialty retailers (LootCrate, Busted Ts, etc.)

Cost Structure	Revenue Streams
Customer Acquisition Costs: Free promotion (organic) *Distribution costs*: Free (YouTube) *Hosting*: $20 a month *People*: Host does everything.	*Revenue Model*: AdWords for Video, Brand deals, affiliate link programs, t-shirt sales. *Life Time Value*: TBD

PRODUCT   MARKET

Understand Business Models and Customer Development

You must know the profile of the audience by segment. What they do / do not like, what other types of videos they currently watch, what other products they are interested in.

It isn't just "video gamers" who are the audience for The RPG Fanatic Show; it is fans of specific game titles and the specific types of content they are searching for related to those games.

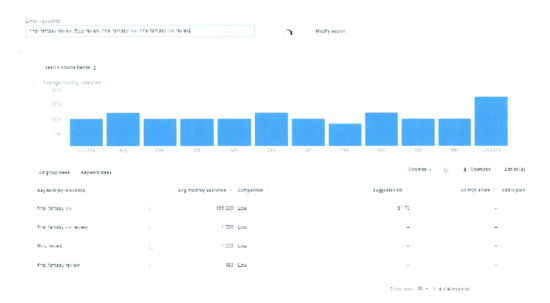

An example of monthly searches for content related to the game Final Fantasy XIV. This shows the precise number of people looking for reviews of the game.

You can do a lot of research using tools (such as AdWords Keyword Planner) to identify the specific keywords your audience uses to find the videos you will be creating, and to gauge the number of people who fit into those segments.

Build the YouTube Equivalent of an MVP

Create your MVF (Minimal Viable Format): This is the video format that is the absolute cheapest you can produce that satisfies the audience. This is also a format that can allows you to consistently produce new videos every week at the same quality level.

Build Relationships with the Audience

Everyone is not your audience. Focus on an identifiable niche with a large enough audience pool to sustain your business. That is what successful entrepreneurs do. You have to tailor your message for a particular kind of person.

Audience Development Funnel

YouTube channels are a business like any other; you have to understand the conversion funnel process in order to fully optimize your efforts and be successful as a small business owner.
The conversion funnel for YouTube content owners looks like this:

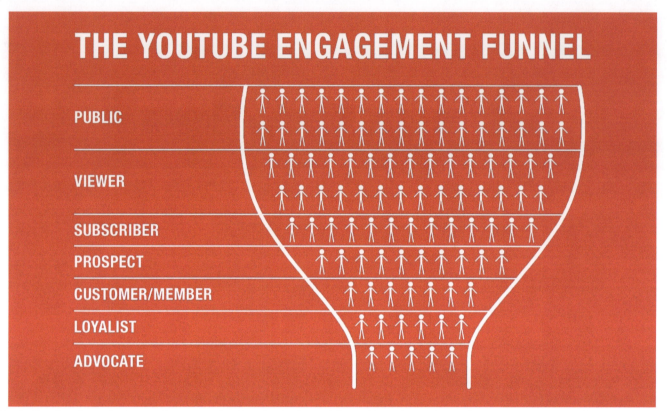

Let's talk about each type of person in the funnel, and how they transform from one type to the next.

Public: This is anyone who sees your video but has not watched it. Your video can be discovered in search engine results like Google, Bing or YouTube. They may also see the video on Facebook or Twitter, or embedded into a blog.

The main thing that will determine whether someone clicks on your video or not is the relevancy of your video thumbnail to the interests of the person. If the video thumbnail does not provide enough information to convince the person that the video will be interesting to them, they won't click on your video. This is why having good custom thumbnails for your video is so important.

You must understand that to get a single viewer, it takes a lot of people just seeing your video thumbnail. The majority of the Public will not watch your video, so you need to market your video heavily to get views to it.

Viewer: This is anyone who has watched your video. They were successfully convinced to click because of the information in your video thumbnail, and are now watching your video.

Whether the person watches your entire video or not depends on only one factor; how well your video delivers on the promise that your video thumbnail image gave. For example, if your video thumbnail is of a beautiful woman but your video is of a dude talking, you will probably lose your viewer immediately. This is because the thumbnail promised a video of a woman, not a man. This is why misleading thumbnails and video titles are a bad tactic to use.

Subscriber: This is a person who watched your video as a Viewer and decided to subscribe to your channel. This person took the effort to log into YouTube and then click the subscribe button because they want to see

An example of an effective video thumbnail is shown above.

more videos from you in the future. Every subscriber is someone who is voting **"I like your content."** They are giving you permission to contact them about new videos and other information. They want you to engage with them.

To facilitate the conversion of a Viewer into a Subscriber, you should have Calls to Action in your videos, usually at the end of the video is what is known as an end-slate. An example of an effective end-slate for converting subscribers is shown below.

Prospect: The Prospect is a Subscriber who has the financial means to buy the products advertised in your videos, or related merchandise from you. To determine whether someone is a Prospect, you must pay attention to their comments. For example, if you are making a video game review and the person says that they are going to buy that game, they have now identified themselves as a Prospect.

If possible, you should keep Prospects in their own G+ Circle using the Insights tool of your YouTube Dashboard (only available to channels over 1,000 subscribers). This enables you to send them videos and information designed to convince them to sign up for a mailing list, through which you can directly offer them products.

Customer / Member: This is a Prospect who has decided to make a purchase decision based on your videos. They have bought a product advertised by a sponsor in your video, or they have purchased something directly from you like a t-shirt or an eBook.

They might also be a Member (someone who is opting into your mailing list, and following you on all social media profiles like Facebook and Twitter). They might even be on your website forum.

This is one of your most valuable types of subscriber and the type of person you must cater to. Keeping these people happy is key to getting them to convert to the next two phases.

Loyalist: This is a Customer who loves everything about your brand. They will watch every video you make, always fund your crowdfunding campaigns, and regularly make purchase decisions based on your endorsement. They make up a small part of your total subscriber base, but they are the second most valuable to an...

Advocate: This is the most important type of subscriber. This person **LOVES** you, because your work has made a meaningful impact in their own lives. They not only make purchase decisions based on you and watch all of your videos, but they regularly encourage other people to become Viewers.

The Advocate helps you advertise your videos by sharing them (not just on Facebook) and also making personal recommendations to their friends. They plug your channel on website forums at the first chance they get in topics about great YouTube channels.

The Advocate is the person who will buy convention tickets just to meet you in person. They want your autograph.

The Advocate makes up the smallest percentage of your audience, but they are by far the most important.

What Is the Product in the Funnel?

The video itself is a product in the sense that you need to sell viewers on the reason to watch your video, **but the video doesn't generate money.**

The Product for your channel is the business model behind it.

What generates money for your channel is sales of related merchandise to your videos (like t-shirts) and the ads that appear on your videos. These are the products you need to sell, and as you can see from the previous chart, it is a process to convert a viewer into a loyal brand advocate.

I have seen some YouTubers, in response to complaints about ads from a vocal minority, encourage their viewers to download ad blocking software. **Don't do that.** Again, you want to run a business. If people won't watch your ads then they are not customers. It is best to ignore these types of people.

You must learn to filter out criticism from the Viewers and Subscribers who will never convert into a Customer. Your goal should not be to have everyone like you on YouTube. That is impossible.

Your goal should be to build a sustainable business from the people who appreciate your work enough to support your career as a content creator.

Don't help people deny your right to be paid for your work by encouraging them to use ad blocking software. That is counter-productive.

How Do I Convert One Type of Audience to the Next?

- Regularly release videos that reinforce your brand. Your video content must belong to the same niche. For example, if you make beauty tutorials then you must continue to make videos of interest to people who like beauty tutorials (like hair style or makeup tutorials).

  If you make videos about book reviews, try to focus on a particular genre like sci-fi or fantasy.
  If you make gaming videos, keep making videos about the types of games getting the most views (shooters, RPGs, puzzle games, etc).

  You can make videos about other topics, but the bulk of your content must be focused on the type of content your audience is most interested in seeing from YOU.

- The quality of your videos must always be rising, never declining. You cannot make one video with top-of-the-line professional After Effects motion graphics, and then make another video with title cards you made in MS Paint. Always improve your production values. The audience will be upset if your quality drops.

- Engage with everyone who comments on your videos. Even if it is a negative comment, you should engage with them as much as humanly possible. This is especially important to do when you are big. Again, you want to engage to convert subscribers into people who will become your top brand advocates.

  You need to grow a KISS Army type of group; a fan club. You cannot do that if you don't engage with people. Even engaging with the haters will show your fans that you are a real person who genuinely wants to respond to everyone.

- Build a website. It is hard to do things like get people to signup to mailing lists or buy your merchandise if you don't operate a website that makes the process easy for them.

  I would not recommend using cheap auto-template sites like Wixx for your website. You can get cheap hosting for as low as $10 a month for a WordPress site, and purchase your own domain name for as cheap as $15 per year. With a WordPress site, you'll be able to install plugins (like content lockers) that convince people to either follow your social profile or sign up for an email list.

An example of a content locker for social media engagement AND mailing list signups is viewable at my own website. I have a special offer page at http://careymartell.com/lean-channel-supplements/ that requires you to take a social action in order to get access to supplemental material. During the sign up process, the student also shares their email address, opting into my mailing list.

This is a general article on the process of audience development for a YouTube channel; but after reading it, you should have the general idea down. I hope that this article helps you!

Section 8. YouTube Terminology

Glossary of YouTube Terminology

The following is a general guide to many of the terms that you will see in this course, and will hear when interacting with other YouTubers.

Annotations: Video Annotations is a way for you to add interactive commentary to your videos. You control what the annotations say, where they appear on the video, and when they appear/disappear. Annotations can also be clicked on to direct the viewer to watch additional videos, or to link to related websites.

Banners: A YouTube banner is the space on top of a channel that is Partnered. Banners allow the channel the ability to have links on the banner to any social media platform or website of the user's choice, as well as offering additional branding functions. Banners have image mapping functions.

Back-link: Backlinks are incoming links to a website or web page. Backlinks are important to place in your YouTube video description field to link social media pages or websites.

Bumps: Also called a "bumper", bumps are 30-60 second segments that either are comedic or informational. (sometimes advertisement). AdultSwim is well known for its nonsensical bumps.

Closed Captions: YouTube videos now include a "CC" button that, if pressed, will automatically generate the closed-captioning technology. (this will help with Keywords)

Channel Watch Page: Every video on YouTube has a "Channel watch page". This is the page where you will generally see a YouTube channel banner and a list of videos from that creator.

Content I.D: YouTube has created an advanced set of copyright policies and content management tools to give rights holders control of their content. YouTube provides content management solutions for rights holders of all sizes across the world, and provides tools to cater to the specific needs of various rights owners.

Copyright strike: YouTube removes content when they receive complete and valid removal requests. When content is removed, a strike is applied to the uploader's account. (If you receive three copyright strikes, your account will be suspended)

Production Bible: This book is a list of all information related to a film, video, or web series. The "bible" is intended to provide a useful, best-practices guide to the thinking, planning, documentation and supporting materials required when developing a property across multiple media platforms. We often create production bibles for complicated film shoots in order to demonstrate to the client what we will do, and to document the progress that we make.

Thumbnail: A thumbnail is a small picture which represents your video on YouTube. After your video has been successfully uploaded, three representative video thumbnails will be generated automatically by the system. Once these thumbnails have been generated, you can select one of the them as your video thumbnail.

Transcript: Transcript files are used to create closed captions for YouTube videos. A transcript file must be saved as a plain text file without any special characters like smart quotes or dashes.

Image Mapping: An image map is a list of coordinates relating to a specific image or video; it is created in order to hyperlink areas of the image or video to various destinations. Youtube banners have image mapping, and Youtube annotations are a type of image map.

Video Manager: The YouTube Video Manager allows you to handle all your uploaded videos, and edit aspects about them such as the video descriptions.

Video: A recording produced with a video recorder (camcorder) or some other device that captures full motion. Video is a different recording medium than "film" because video is digital; film requires recording to film projector tape.

Video Description Field: Video description field (also known as the Description bar) is a good place to put links to any web site. It is also great for writing a description for the video that is playing.

Video Watch Page: The video watch page is the most common place that a YouTube video will be watched. Related video feeds, user comments and video description can all be accessed through the video watch page.

MODULE II. SCREENWRITING

Section 1. Why Write a Screenplay?

I have met many YouTubers that do not write screenplays for their productions; they simply get an idea, grab a camera, and improvise the entire thing. That can work very well, but sometimes you want to make videos with *other* people, and do some technical things like fight scenes or special effects that require a lot of communication between the people filming the scene.

If you plan to shoot videos with other people, having a screenplay will make filming much smoother. The screenplay functions as a step by step guide on what needs to happen in every scene, and will be used by everyone to do their job. Actors need to have context for their lines so that they can understand the motivations of a character, and the cinematographers need to block out a scene so that they can film it in the most ideal setting to invoke the appropriate mood.

Screenwriting is a very detailed craft and if you are serious about the topic, you should either enroll into a film school or read a lot of books on the subject. We'll briefly talk about how to write a screenplay, because I believe this knowledge is invaluable for creators who are serious about being professional.

PS: If you're going to buy some books on writing, these are the books I recommend.
A good story, whether fiction or non-fiction, has four essential things.

* Plot
* Characters
* Conflict
* Theme

Let's dissect each aspect in more detail.

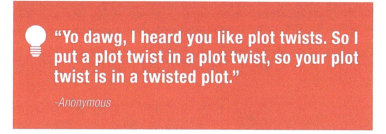

Section 2. Elements of a Narrative

Plot

The plot is the flow of the story itself, the way it unfolds from start to finish.

A basic plot has the following phases to its structure:

Introduction: The beginning of the story where the characters and the setting is revealed.

Rising Action: This is where the events in the story become complicated and the conflict in the story is revealed (events between the introduction and climax).

Climax: This is the highest point of interest and the turning point of the story. The reader wonders what will happen next; will the conflict be resolved or not?

Falling Action: The events and complications begin to resolve themselves. The reader knows what has happened next and if the conflict was resolved or not (events between climax and resolution).

Resolution: The part of the plot that concludes the falling action by revealing or suggesting the outcome of the conflict.

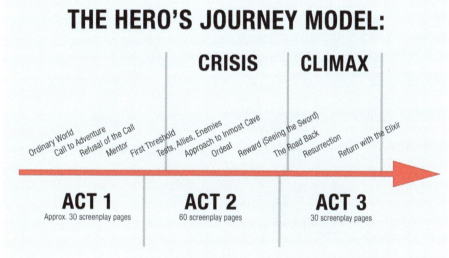

'Monomyth' has an elaborate structure, breaking up the elements of a Plot into many smaller parts.

Characters

You can find general archetypes for characters in Joseph Campbell's monomyth structure, but you can also find more laser-focused archetypes by searching **TV Tropes**.

If you'd like to learn in detail how to write a screenplay in the monomyth style, check out The Writer's Journey: Mythic Structure for Writers. You can order it through Amazon.

Conflict

Conflict is a basic problem for the characters to overcome in a story, it's the driving force. If you don't have conflict, then you don't have a story

There are seven basic types of conflicts in a story:

1. **Man vs. Man,**
2. **Man vs. Self.**
3. **Man vs. Nature**
4. **Man vs. Society.**
5. **Man vs. God/Fate**
6. **Man caught in the Middle,** of other characters/conflicts.
7. **Male vs. Female.**

Theme

Themes are what stories are about; the philosophy, message, or idea at the heart of a story.

Stories are told for two reasons: entertainment and education.

In essence, this is what separates reality from fiction: real life has no central theme, no message or great meaning, save the one that we transpose on it ourselves.

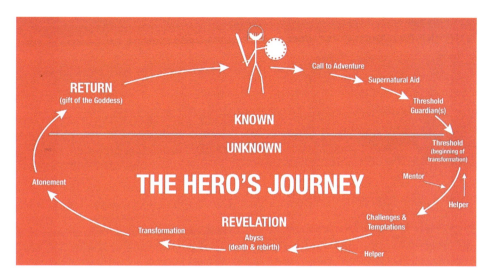

Section 3. Monomyth Narrative Structure

How to Write a Screenplay Using Joseph Campbell's Hero's Journey Model (Monomyth)

Monomyth can be defined as a story structure model that is based on the writings of Joseph Campbell. It is designed to be a guide so that people can write an effective screenplay that will hit all the of important emotional buttons in a person, and will keep them engaged in the plot.

Monomyth screenplays deliver a universal model of psychological maturation or spiritual journey to the audience. In other words, all of the people in the audience will be able to see themselves in the story through the character. This will assist the audience in gaining personal insights into their own lives.

In this article, you will find a basic overview on how to write a screenplay using the monomyth plot structure.

Act 1: Separation / Departure

In the first part, the hero makes the decision of whether he should participate further in the story or not. This process can also be defined as the "separation of hero from normal world."

I.1 The Call to Adventure – In this stage, the hero is introduced to the world. This is where the hero begins the story. Moreover, the hero is asked to embark on the adventure.

I.2 Refusal of the Call – There are instances where the hero refuses to go on the adventure. If the hero does refuse to go on the adventure, this is where the story develops.
Acceptance of the Call

I.3 Supernatural Aid – If the hero does not refuse to go on the adventure, the first encounter has to happen. According to Campbell, this initial encounter is with a protective figure.

I.4 Crossing of the First Threshold – At this point, the hero is ready to make his first step on the path. The hero gets out of his comfort zone (such as his home) to go in search of adventure. This scene is usually associated with anxiety because the hero is unsure about the things that are coming his way.

I.5 Entering the Belly of the Whale – The hero takes the first step out of his comfort zone.

Act 2 : The Victories and Trials of Initiation

II.1 Road of Trials – Now the adventure has started. This is the beginning of the second phase, and the hero goes through an unknown landscape. A lot of challenges are coming his way, and he will have to fight with them.

II.2 The Meeting with the Goddess – The hero meets the Goddess of myth in this stage. However, the hero should be in a state to accept the Goddess.

II.3 Woman as Temptress – There are some heroes who see it as an ultimate ordeal to resist an inappropriate lover. Moreover, the hero should visit the Goddess in an appropriate manner to be accepted.

II.4 Atonement with the Father – The hero must confront a parental or authority figure with whom they have a difficult relationship or conflict. This figure is rarely an actual person, but more often a god, or sometimes a concept or force of nature. This figure must be defeated or persuaded, or the hero must win their approval in some way in order to progress in the story.

II.5 Apotheosis – The hero is transforming from a child into an adult. The hero might obtain his own family, or possibly an extended family through association with a group of loyal allies. He might also suffer a terrible blow or weakness that causes him to become more frail and mundane, and less youthful.

II.6 The Ultimate Boon – The hero achieves a great victory, successfully accomplishing the task he set out to do. This is followed by celebration. The hero gets his first taste of true success.

Act 3: Reintegration and Return with Society

After achieving the triumph, the hero returns back to the place he began. The journey is depicted in this stage.

III.1 Refusal of the Return – Sometimes the hero may think that he doesn't want to return back to his old life. In that kind of a situation, he either remains where he is, or tries to hide, believing he will return after everything is solved. But he never returns.

III.2 Magic Flight – If the hero wins and makes the decision to come back, this stage comes into play. During this final stage of the adventure, all of the powers and skills that he obtained on his journey are being used.

III.3 Rescue from Without – There are instances where the hero would stay in his other world with pleasure. However, it will not be a wise choice when considered in the long run. The society that he belongs to may want him to celebrate what he has achieved. Therefore, his allies will make the decision to go out, to rescue the hero, and to bring him back home.

III.4 Crossing of the Return Threshold – The hero will have to cross the borders between two worlds one more time when returning back home. However, he will have to give up some of the powers that he has earned. This can even be the lover that he has won. Rarely are there lucky heroes who will have two homes in both worlds, so they do not find it as a big issue when crossing.

III.5 Master of the Two Worlds – This is where the hero makes both worlds his home. In this kind of situation, the hero will not have to give up his powers when crossing the border. He will also get the opportunity to keep his lover forever.

III.6 Freedom to Live – After achieving victory, the hero has to settle down in the world. Now all the issues that set him on his journey have been resolved, and it is time for the hero to rest. He has contributed a lot towards curing his world through the powers he has won. This is the stage where the reader gets to know about the final outcome of the journey. The hero has gone through a lot of issues, and finally it is the time for him to settle down with his family and friends, and to live a normal life.

This kind of monomyth is associated with a happy ending. In this type of story, children will have to become adults and they will have to face a lot of issues that adults encounter. It is up to them to go through those issues and create a better future. If they can create it, they will receive the opportunity to live happily for the rest of their lives.

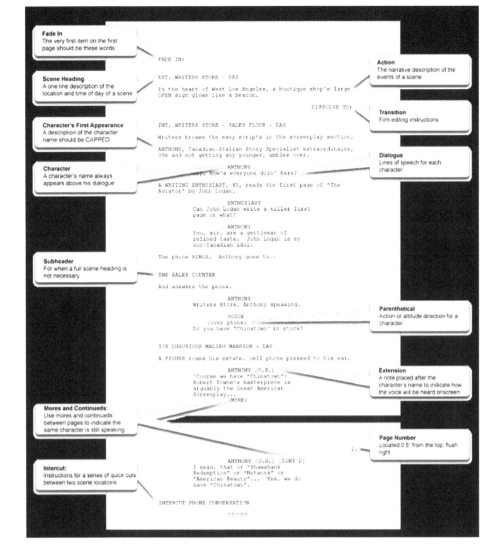

Section 4. How to Structure a Screenplay

A screenplay is different from any other written piece, and there are some aspects that you need to be aware of when starting to compose a screenplay.

If you are a novice in this area, then reading a couple of screenplays would really help in giving you an overall idea about how your own should look like. Study all of its feature and see how everything is structured.

While a novel is usually based on describing every aspect of the story and providing the narration for it, a screenplay is a bit different. It is about highlighting the tips of putting a story into a scene, the indications for the setting, the lines for every actor, and the details of how the action unfolds in the future movie. The story is told in an audio-visual way, and the screenplay is the instruction for how this information must be depicted by the cast and crew.

Formatting

When composing the first page of the script, the first words that should be put down are **"fade in,"** and then everything else will follow.

A very important aspect that you should remember is not to number the first page. Page numbering will begin with the second page, and will appear in the right upper corner of the page, at a 0.5'' placement from the top of the page and close to the margins on the right.

Another aspect that you should know about is **spacing**. The top and bottom margins of the page must be 1'' and the margins for the left should be 1.5''. The extra space will help in binding the document with brads.

For the entire document, you should use single spacing while writing.

A screenplay should always begin with presenting the scene where the action is happening. The scene heading should be written in caps and will be only one line, which will present the location and the general time of the day (morning, evening, night, etc). This particular line will have the name of **"slugline"**. If there is the need to make some specifications regarding aspects of the scene, but there is no need in starting a new scene heading, you may use a subheader to point them out.

Also use the term **"intercut"** when you want to introduce quick changes within the scene and mention the location where everything is taking place.

The action in a screenplay should always be written in the present tense. Do not introduce inner monologues or thoughts of the supporting characters. While this works well for a novel, it can bring disaster for most screenplays that are centered around a single character. Only write the things that can be seen or heard by the character; this will ensure that the character will know how to play that certain scene. When you introduce the character in the action, make sure that his or her name is written with capital letters and maybe a short description of his or her personality or attitude. Also include a note written in parentheses to indicate how his voice should be heard in the set. This is called as an **"extension"**; it tells the actors, director and editor if the dialogue is meant to be Off-camera (O.S.), Off-screen (O.F.) or as a Voice-over (V.O.).

If there are any other minor characters that participate in the action of the scene, they can be mentioned without a name, but in a word that describe their role, like "neighbor" or "taxi driver."

The dialog format as shown in the above image should be used every time the characters have something to say, even in the cases of voice-overs or off-screen situations. Center your dialogue beneath the centered extensions and character name.

Another aspect to include in a screenplay is the **transition**, meaning you will give editing instructions for how the frames of the film are to be arranged. These transitions will be marked with verbs like **"dissolve to,"** **"cut to,"** **"smash cut,"** **"quick cut"** or **"fade to."** These are used to show how time has passed or to transition between characters and other indications that you might consider necessary. Specifying a shot is another detail that you should include in a screenplay; mention the focal point. But this specification should be used only if you want to. Creating the shot list for each scene is normally the job of the director.

Again, this is general advice. If you want to master the form, the I suggest reading a book on screenwriting or enrolling into a screenwriting workshop.

Screenwriting Software

There are two main software suits that people use: Final Draft and Celtx.

Final Draft is industry standard but expensive, but *Celtx* is cheaper.

I recommend Celtx, but it is your choice.

Master the Art of Story-telling and You'll Go Far

MODULE III. VIDEO PRODUCTION

Look at the above picture. Memorize it. *Embrace it*. Now hate it. This triangle is your nemesis as a YouTuber and it will be thwarting your best laid plans at every possible opportunity.

Unlike a Hollywood production, you never have enough time, money or manpower to make the "perfect" film. You will always be cutting corners somewhere.

You have to decide if you want your videos to look nice, or if it's okay to just look passable.

To be perfectly honest, I would need 100+ pages to teach you how to operate a camera. Film-making is the art of painting with light, and there are a lot of theories to learn. So I'm going to suggest that you read the following books to learn how to be a cinematographer.

But I will give you some general tips.

Tips for Operating a Video Camera

First of all, inspect your video camera before turning it on. This means that you should examine it on every side, press all of the buttons, flip the screen in and out to get familiar with the movement, and adjust its straps to make it most comfortable for you. You should also see where the on and off button is placed and become familiar with its position. This is because some video cameras have the recording button in the same spot.

Video cameras are equipped with batteries or custom made accumulators. Make sure you know which kind your camera needs, and practice the operation of taking them out and replacing them until you feel comfortable with it. Also, check to see where the tape or memory cards go in. When you shoot videos and run out of memory, it will be a great thing to know where to replace the storage unit for your device.

Another thing that you should do is become familiar with how things look through the camera's lens. Take the cap off and try looking through it. Play around with the zoom functions, and see the maximum and minimum points for them. Try them out with some test footage; shoot some walking shots and scenery around you. Most video cameras have an automatic focus setting, and this setting will adjust the camera according to external factors. But with a little attention and by following the advice in the user's manual, you will be able to manually adjust the settings you consider important.

Regarding the use of natural or artificial lighting, here is some advice to help you capture the best shots.

If you are filming inside, but you have a window near you with a great amount of light coming in, the best position to assume is by placing your back to the window. The light will pour in from behind you and light your scene or subject, offering the best view.

If you aim your camera directly at a light source, you risk having a burned image. The camera will focus on the brightest points of the image and the subject will appear in the video as a dark silhouette.

You should follow the above advice when you are outside and there is plenty of sun. Always turn with your back against the sun and try to use its light to "paint" the scene, object or person you want to capture on tape. Aiming your camera towards the direction of the sun will only get you **over-exposed** shots that are "too hot", and appear to be poor quality.

If you want to continue filming while the sun sets and the natural light is decreasing, consider getting some artificial lighting. This will also be placed behind the video camera and towards your scene. I recommend that you have your lights sit at least three feet away from the main subject. The will better ensure the best shot scenes and that there are no over-exposed areas on the subject's face due to the lights being too close to their skin.

Framing is also an important aspect, if you want your shoots to be good. Try to ignore the natural instinctive feeling that the subject of the shot must be in the center of the screen. This only looks great if you're making a close-up shoot.

There are a few simple rules to apply when framing a scene: look for lines in your frame (vertical or horizontal) that will help you make the best framing. You must take into consideration the rule of thirds. This is best described as splitting the screen into nine equal sections. These lines or points of main interest are placed at the intersection of the first third or second third of the lines, and not in the center of the screen. When you are filming a wider shot, you should always leave an empty space (also called **"head room"**)

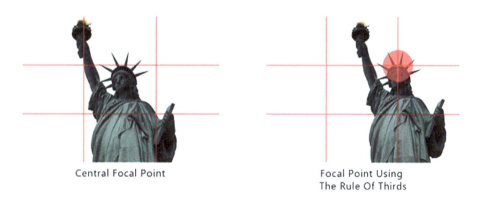

Central Focal Point

Focal Point Using
The Rule Of Thirds

An example of the Rule of Thirds in execution.

for your main character, in the direction where their attention is going to. This will add some substance and depth to your scene. To avoid bad cuts (like having and image of a half person or half objects) always pay attention to your frame's edges.

Lastly, you should know that most video cameras have a built-in microphone that will help you capture all of the sound in the area around you, even the noises that your brain filters out like a running air conditioner or refrigerator. You may not be aware of these noises until after the shoot, because you were too focused on that acting or filming. This is something to be aware of; try to choose a location in which you can control the sound pollution. Don not film by the side of a busy high-way or another noisy place; the audio you record will be useless to you.

You might also consider making a boom pole and purchasing a shotgun mic to record your audio separate from your camera's built-in microphone.

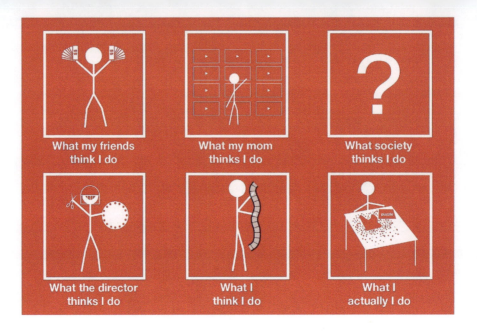

What my friends
think I do

What my mom
thinks I do

What society
thinks I do

What the director
thinks I do

What I
think I do

What I
actually I do

Section 2. Editing a Video

For the purposes of this online course, we will also talk about video editing during this video production module, even though it is usually discussed in its own topic, "post-production."

The easiest way to learn how to edit videos is by writing down all the scenes of your screenplay onto index cards, and then laying these index cards out on a table in front you. Think about each index card as one raw, unedited video file, and move the scenes around to make your story.

This is exactly how a non-linear video editing program works. Each raw video file from your camera is just an index card that you can drag around the timeline of your editing software to organize your master video and assemble the story into a sequence. In a way, it is like putting together a jigsaw puzzle.

How to Edit a YouTube Video

To create and edit a video for YouTube is not as difficult as it may seem. You just need a simple video editing program that usually comes installed on your computer when you purchase it. If not, you also have the possibility of using the editing tools that YouTube has available for its users.

Software like Windows Movie Maker is all that you need in order to get started and prepare a video suitable for viewing on YouTube. I do recommend purchasing something like Sony Vegas, Final Cut Pro or Adobe Premiere if you want to have the full range of options available to a non-linear editor, but Windows Movie Maker / iMovie will work just fine for a beginner.

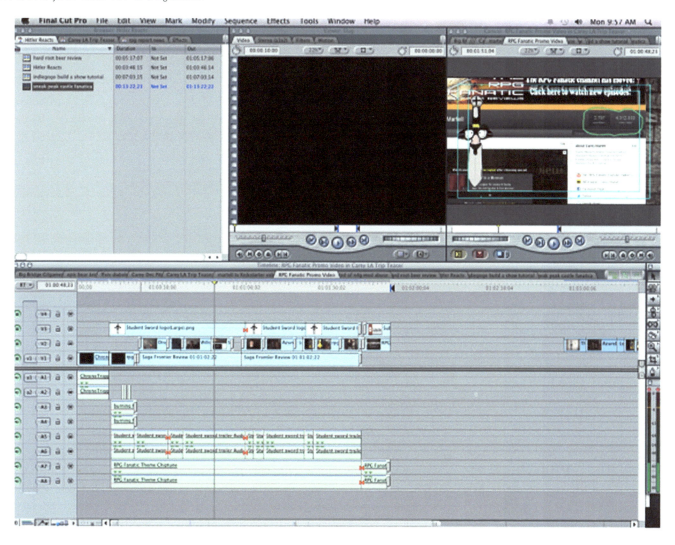

A timeline in Final Cut Pro. Notice there are many layers of video footage (blue segments) sitting above the music and sound files (green footage). This is how all NLE's look.

With the help of the video editing program, you can use pictures or footage made by you to create the movie that you want. You can also choose to add music to it. The program should have an import button where you can add pictures or video in a certain order, whichever you prefer, so that the movie will play in a cinematic way that audiences have become accustomed to. Editing programs usually have two different lines for pictures and music; if you choose to add music, you can put it in a parallel line with the images and play them both at same time so that their elements merge into a single scene. This will allow you to create a perfect soundtrack for your video, and insert sound effects.

You also have the option of making different cuts while you work on the video. You can delete, cut or adjust anything that you think is out of order. If you are using any of the more expensive editors I recommended, there are several effects or filters that you can add to make your video more spectacular (like altering the colors or adding lens flare effects).

Just play around and see what fits best. Video computers allow for "non-destructive" editing, which means if you screw up you can just click the Undo option on the program. Don't be afraid of the canvas - experiment!

When you feel that your work is finished and everything is as you want it to be, close this process by choosing to publish the video or save it on your computer.

Exporting Your Video File

In general, YouTube accepts videos that have a resolution of 1920 x 1080 pixels. Higher resolutions present no problems, other than the fact that it may require a longer time to load or upload.

In file size, the maximum video length is one gigabyte and 15 minutes in time duration for non-YouTube Partner accounts. Only YouTube Partners are permitted to exceed these limits.

When saving your finished video, take into consideration the types of container formats that YouTube accepts in uploading video: WMV, AVI, MOV, and MPG.

The video compression format that you should use for all of your video exports is *H.264.* This is what YouTube likes the best and I do not recommend anything else.

Section 3. Your Video Intro

Your intro is often the very first thing that audiences see when they watch your video.

Traditionally, the "intro" is called opening title sequence, and that is the correct industry term for this necessary part of your video.

Ideally your intro should be no longer than 3-6 seconds. Long intros tend to not work as well on YouTube, unless the intros themselves are very unique and can keep the audience interested. Remember, if you lose the interest of your audience, it is very easy for them to click on a video from the Related videos feed, and it may not be one of your videos that they go to.

Although we call it the intro, it can often times be better to start a video without your show's opening sequence. When you start out with a brand new YouTube channel where no one knows your show, it is especially better to begin your video in medias res, or in the midst of action. An example would be starting a video featuring pranks with a short 3-4 second clip of people reacting dramatically to the prank. It is then followed by your intro sequence, which then rolls into the host explaining what prank is going to be done, and showing the setup of that prank.

In any case, the intro to your video is necessary to help brand your videos. The intro also allows audiences to be sure that they are watching the right video: your video. A consistent opening title sequence allows the audience to be sure that they are watching a video that you produced.

Section 4. Your Video Outro (also called an End Slate)

Call to Action End-Slate / Video "Outro"

Having a good outro at the end of your video that asks the audience to do something (i.e. like, subscribe, share or comment on the video) is crucial. It's best if you ask them to do something specific that allows them to add their own personality to it. For example, I started asking people to tell me who their favorite characters were. You can see what that engagement end-slate looks like by clicking on my *Hyperdimension Neptunia Victory review* (I've set the link to go directly to the end of the video).

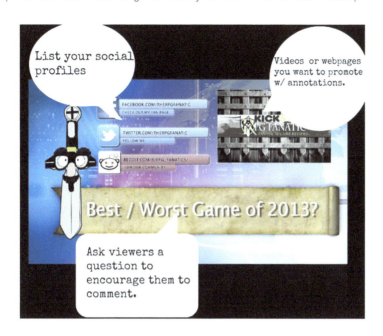

Anatomy of a Good YouTube End-slate

Example of a good end-slate from an episode of The RPG Report.

The increased engagement helps the video get re-shared to the G+ , Twitter and Facebook profiles that they have integrated with YouTube. It also sends social signals to the search engines that the video is something to pay attention to. For those reasons, all of your videos should have an outro.

How to Make an End-Slate / Outro

You can do it several ways; a stand-alone image file or a video created in After Effects. Either route is fine. I do think that After Effects templates are more visually interesting.

Want some free YouTube end-slate and thumbnail .psd files?

I have created a .zip file that contains:

1.   YouTube end-slate (outro) template .psd file
2.   YouTube video thumbnail template .psd file

By modifying the Adobe Photoshop .psd templates, you can create your own YouTube video end slates and thumbnails for your channel. All you have to do is remove the placeholder art and replace it with your own. You can also modify the backgrounds and positions of different elements. It's a great foundation to start with.

To download the files, go to: http://careymartell.com/lean-channel-supplements/

Section 5. Fair Use and Cover Songs on YouTube

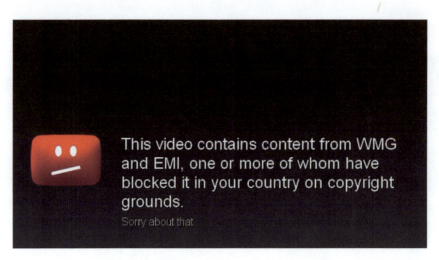

If you use music that you do not have a right to use in your videos, you'll probably see this.

As YouTube gets bigger, Google has been working out deals with major companies to make more money. Some of these deals involve how Google interprets "Fair Use" on YouTube.

The most important thing that people need to understand about YouTube is that it is a privately held corporation, and it is free to decide what content it will and won't monetize as on its own policies!

By contrast, "fair use" is a legal doctrine intended as a defense against a lawsuit.

If no one is suing you, "fair use" is simply not applicable!

Despite what you may have heard, inserting something like, "This video is a review and is protected by the fair-use policy and was made for educational purposes" provides you **absolutely zero protection from your video being disabled!**

The reason is this: because it is not cost effective to sue millions of people who upload copyrighted material, major corporations are working out agreements with YouTube to ensure that they don't have to file lawsuits to have copyright infringement removed from YouTube. This means it becomes very important to comply with Youtube's policies concerning the use of material that you don't own in your videos, which is described at *http://www.youtube.com/t/copyright_permissions*

YouTube has a feature called *Content ID* that data-mines all YouTube videos, looking for audio that matches registered works from major music publishers. If it finds a match, YouTube flags that video for monetization by the owner of the music, and gives them the right to also delete the video from YouTube.

A Content ID match will not necessarily penalize your account. It will only penalize you if you get a copyright strike.

Do I need a license to do cover songs?

If you are interested in making a cover song or song parody, it would behoove you to obtain a license for the song. Without a license, a Content ID claim will probably get filed on your video eventually, or a publisher may even request that your video be deleted. This will leave you with a copyright strike. If you get a copyright strike, you will lose your YouTube Partnership.

That said, many song-writers and singers have been able to grow their own audiences by doing cover songs. This is because YouTubers search for songs they already know, rather than wholly original work made by unknown singers. It can be an effect strategy for singers starting out to do cover songs and accept a Content ID Match in exchange for the potential to grow a big audience. It is very risky though, as you may receive a copyright strike while doing this. The choice is up to you.

Quiz Questions: Fair Use & Content ID

1. What is Content ID?
   A. A cool new band
   B. A feature that YouTube uses to find music and movies belonging to major publishers and monetize the videos on behalf of these companies.

2. Uploading cover songs without having a license from the owner of the song is fair use. (True / False)

3. If I get a copyright strike, I will lose my YouTube Partnership status. (True / False)

4. If I get a Content ID Match, I will lose my YouTube Partnership status. (True / False)

5. Doing cover songs on YouTube can be a good way to grow my audience as a singer, but it comes with risks of copyright strikes. (True / False)

Section 6. Monetizing Gaming Footage

As a YouTube Partner who creates video game reviews on my channel *The RPG Fanatic*, I am frequently asked about whether making video game reviews is allowed to be monetized or not.

The above video explains *YouTube's policy concerning video game footage and fair use*. This is important information to know because unless you have permission from a developer to use gameplay footage in your videos, you must abide by YouTube's fair use policy for videogame footage.

YouTube's policy is very strict. They will not allow you to place ads on gameplay if there are no audio commentary tracks you have created yourself, and your commentary must provide educational or instructional value.

This means that you cannot just upload video game trailers and expect to make money; YouTube won't allow you to do that.

For more information about fair use and DMCA on YouTube, please check the following links:

Using some copyrighted content in your video:

http://www.google.com/support/youtube/bin/answer.py?answer=143457

Youtube Video Monetization checklist:

http://support.google.com/youtube/bin/answer.py?hl=en&answer=2490020

Partner Help Center: Video Game and Software Content

http://www.google.com/support/youtube/bin/answer.py?hl=en&answer=138161

Center for Social Media: Fair Use for Documentary & Online Video Makers

http://www.centerforsocialmedia.org/fair-use

Section 7. Film Crew Positions Glossary

Glossary of Film Crew Positions

The following is an introduction to many of the positions on a TV or movie production. Although you may primarily create videos by yourself today, you will interact with many people in the web video industry who have traditional film backgrounds and/or currently produce content the same way that traditional networks do. It is important to understand these terms so that you know who you are speaking with at events.

Producer

A Film Producer creates the conditions for making movies or videos. The Producer initiates, coordinates, supervises, and controls matters such as raising funding, hiring key personnel, and arranging for distributors. The producer is involved throughout all phases of the filmmaking process, from development to the completion of a project.

Production Manager

The Production Manager supervises the physical aspects of the production (not the creative aspects) including personnel, technology, budget, and scheduling. It is the Production Manager's responsibility to make sure that the filming stays on schedule and within its budget. The PM also helps manage the day-to-day budget by managing operating costs such as salaries, production costs, and everyday equipment rental costs. The PM often works under the supervision of a Producer, and directly supervises the Production Coordinator.

Production Coordinator

The Production Coordinator is the information nexus of the productio; he or she is responsible for organizing all the logistics from hiring crew, renting equipment, and booking talent. The PC is an integral part of film production.

Production Assistant

Production Assistants, referred to as PAs, assist in the production office or in various departments with general tasks, such as assisting the First Assistant Director with set operations.

Screenwriter

The Screenwriter, or Scriptwriter, may pitch a finished script to potential Producers, or may write a script under contract to a Producer. A Writer may be involved, to various degrees, with creative aspects of production.

Script Supervisor

Also known as the continuity person, the Script Supervisor keeps track of what parts of the script have been filmed, and makes notes of any deviations between what was actually filmed and what appeared in the script. They make notes on every shot, and keep track of props, blocking, and other details to ensure continuity from shot to shot and scene to scene. The Script Supervisor's notes are given to the Editor to expedite the editing process. The Script Supervisor works very closely with the Director on set.

Casting Director

The Casting Director chooses the Actors for the characters of the film. This usually involves inviting potential Actors to read an excerpt from the script for an audition.

Director

The Director is responsible for overseeing the creative aspects of a film, including controlling the content and flow of the film's plot, directing the performances of Actors, organizing and selecting the locations in which the film will be shot, and managing technical details such as the positioning of cameras, the use of lighting, and the timing and content of the film's soundtrack. Though directors wield a great deal of power, they are ultimately subordinate to the film's Producer(s). Some Directors, especially more established ones, take on many of the roles of a Producer, and the distinction between the two roles is sometimes blurred.

First Assistant Director

The First Assistant Director (1st AD) assists the Production Manager and Director. The ultimate aim of any 1st AD is to ensure that the film comes in on schedule while maintaining a working environment in which the Director, principal artists (Actors) and crew can be focused on their work. They oversee day-to-day management of the cast and crew scheduling, equipment, script, and set. A 1st AD may also be responsible for directing background action for major shots or the entirety of relatively minor shots, at the Director's discretion.

Second Assistant Director

The Second Assistant Director (2nd AD) is the chief assistant of the 1st AD and helps carry out those tasks delegated to the 1st AD. The 2nd AD may also direct background action and extras in addition to helping the 1st AD with scheduling, booking, etc. The 2nd AD is responsible for creating Call Sheets that let the crew know the schedule and important details about the shooting day. In Canadian and British functional structures, there are 3rd ADs and even Trainee ADs; in the American system there are 2nd 2nd ADs.

Location Scout

The Location Scout does much of the actual research, footwork and photography to document location possibilities. Often the Location Manager will do some scouting himself, as well as the Assistant Location Manager.

Make-up Artist

Make-up Artists work with makeup, hair and special effects to create the characters' look for anyone appearing on screen. Their role is to manipulate an Actor's on-screen appearance whether it makes them look younger, larger, older, or in some cases monstrous. There are also Body Makeup Artists who concentrate their abilities on the body, rather than the head.

Special Effect Supervisor

The Special Effects Supervisor instructs the Special Effects crew on how to design moving set elements and props that will safely break, explode, burn, collapse and implode without destroying the film set. He or she also instructs on building set pieces like breakaway furniture and cities in miniature, lighting pyrotechnics, and on setting up rigging equipment for stunts. They can also assist with prosthetic makeup. He or she is also responsible for reproducing weather conditions and other on-camera magic.

Cinematographer

The term Cinematographer has been a point of contention for some time now. It is usually synonymous with Director of Photography, though some professionals insist that this only applies when the Director of Photography and Camera Operator are the same person.

Boom Operator

The Boom Operator is an assistant to the Production Sound Mixer, and is responsible for microphone placement/movement during filming. The Boom Operator uses a boom pole, a long pole made of light aluminum or carbon fiber that allows precise positioning of the microphone above or below the Actors, just out of the camera's frame. The Boom Operator may also place radio microphones and hidden set microphones.

Film Editor

The Film Editor is the person who assembles the various shots into a coherent film, with the help of the Director. There are usually several Assistant Editors.

Become familar with the roles needed for professional video production in order to produce higher quality shows.

MODULE IV. MARKETING YOUR YOUTUBE CHANNEL

Section 1. YouTube Channel Setup

Now that you've produced a video, let's set up your YouTube channel to match the look and image of your videos.

Make Your Channel Look Good

YouTube has a Creator Academy course specifically designed to help people set up their channels to look nice. It integrates with your channel to help you through the steps. You can find the course here.

The information on this page is meant to be supplementary to the official YouTube information.

Anatomy of a YouTube Channel Front Page

Because some YouTubers struggle with the ideal way to set up their channel's front page, we put together this infographic. Follow this chart to become optimized for engagement and cross-promotion with other YouTubers. We'll use the *Power Up TV YouTube Network channel* as an example.

YouTube Channel Branded Banner and Avatar:

Your banner should have a "call to action" directing your viewers to check out your channel links page. This will increase the click-through rates for you.

YouTube channel banners have an optimal banner image size of 2560 x 1440 pixels.

A template can be downloaded at my website. http://careymartell.com/lean-channel-supplements/

YouTube channel avatars (also called icons) are a square image of 800 X 800 px.

Both your banner and avatar should have consistent branding. The branding should be unique to yourself so that viewers can recognize your channel videos as the official source for those videos. This also will help build brand identity with your audience.

YouTube Channel Featured Links

You will want to include your Facebook, Twitter and Google Plus profiles to make it easy for fans to follow you on these platforms. It is also wise include your website link.

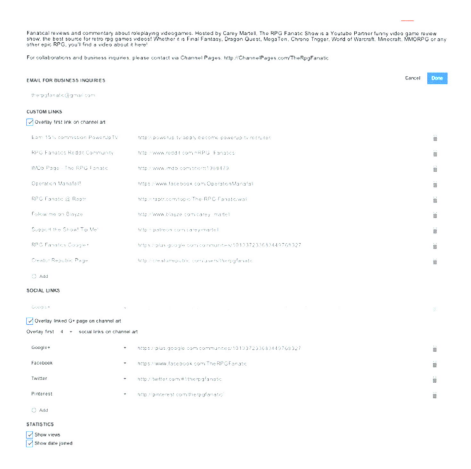

Channel Trailer

Your channel trailer is the first video that a non-subscribed viewer will see when visiting your channel. This video should tell the viewer what they can expect from other videos on your channel, or provide some information about your channel.

The point of the video is to convince the viewer to watch your other videos, to become a subscriber or to take another action that beneficial to you in some way. For example, we have a rap music jingle about the network as our channel trailer.

Featured Channels

This feed exists to the right hand side of your channel trailer. These are channels that are either affiliated with you in some way, or that are cross-promoting with you by including your channel in their own featured feed.

Add other YouTubers that you collaborate / co-promote with to your featured channels feed. Do not add people who won't add you back; find people who will reciprocate that action that you are featuring them.

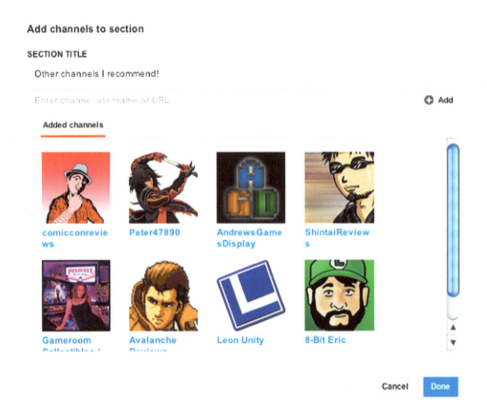

Revent Videos Playlist / Feed

This is a playlist or feed of your most recently uploaded videos. This makes it easy for folks to find your latest videos directly from the front page of your YouTube channel.

Featured Channels Playlist

Your featured channel playlist is another place for your cross-promotion collaborators to be seen by your audience. If you like, you can also make this a playlist featuring their videos.

2ⁿᵈ Playlist

Your 2ⁿᵈ Playlist should have videos about a certain kind of subject or niche. It might be a particular show segment that you produce. On the Power Up TV channel, we have our Creator Academy videos as the 2ⁿᵈ playlist. (We call this is the 2ⁿᵈ playlist because it is the 2ⁿᵈ video playlist on the channel)

Additional Playlists

You should have as many playlists as you can feature on the front page of your channel.

On the Power Up TV channel, we have additional playlists for Testimonials and Sponsorship Winners, as well as a feed showcasing the most popular videos on the channel.

YouTube Video Thumbnails

I used to have passable video thumbnails for the games I reviewed on my channel, and no channel trailer. After producing better channel thumbnails, my videos received more clicks from Google & YouTube Search. My channel trailer also got people asking me questions about which videos I used clips from, which led them to go and watch those videos.

Anatomy of a YouTube Video Thumbnail

Breakdown of the template I use for my show

YouTube Video Description and Tags

Most YouTubers do not do this step properly, yet it's one of the most crucial for your success.

How to Find Keywords for YouTube Video SEO'ing

YouTube is a huge source for traffic; it has over 1 billion unique visitors per month and is the second largest search engine in the world. It is possible to get millions of views from organic (non-paid) search results alone.

But there is one thing that tends to hold creators back: they often do not know how to **S**earch **E**ngine **O**ptimize (SEO) their channel for organic discovery. This is a problem because YouTube is a search engine.

Anyone can make YouTube videos, but the toughest work is in discovering the right keyword combinations that will launch your video into the first spot for high volume search phrases. You can succeed if you follow a few steps, and invest the necessary time to find the right keywords.

How to Find Good YouTube SEO Keywords

In order for your YouTube video to show up in the first search page of Google, you need to find what keywords are favored by YouTube's search algorithms. If you hit the jackpot, Google will spring your video right in the first page of search results. For example, search queries done for subjects that contain the phrase "how to" tend to receive hundreds of thousands of search queries per month (sometimes even millions of searches). People use search engines most often when they are looking up information, which usually comes in the form of tutorials or information about certain subjects, such as...

- sports
- movies
- games
- history
- beauty
- cooking

This is why game reviews and walkthroughs are such a popular niche on YouTube. The videos are information about a subject people are searching for.

Videos that are funny or cute, although popular, get the majority of their views because they are heavily shared by users on social networks. By contrast, "how to" videos tend to not get as many shares, but do receive a lot of search engine traffic from people looking for information.

To understand why is it important to optimize your video with these types of keywords, you must remember that YouTube has NO way of knowing what your video is about unless you provide it text. The fields for Title, Video Description and Tags are used by YouTube to data-mine the video and figure out what it is about, so that when someone searches for a topic like *"Ragnarok Online Review"* your video is the top result.

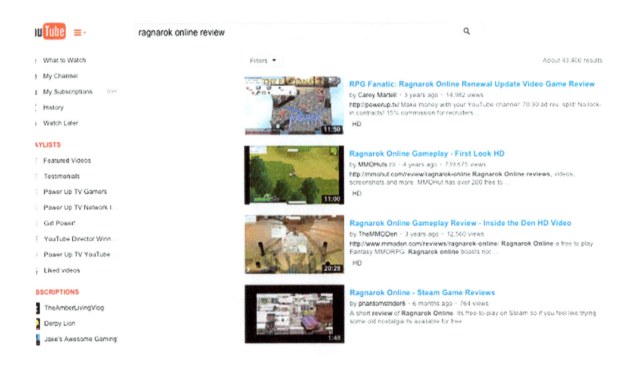

My video review about the game Ragnarok Online is the #1 search result on YouTube because I properly SEOed my video.

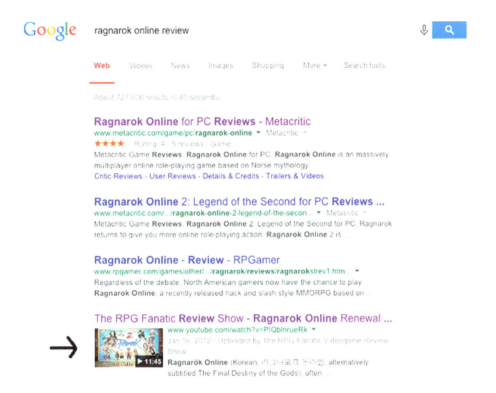

Another of my videos about the game also ranks in a top spot on Google searches for the keyword.

Let's look at what it really means for a video to be in the top spot for a search query, and why this is important for growing your channel's audience.

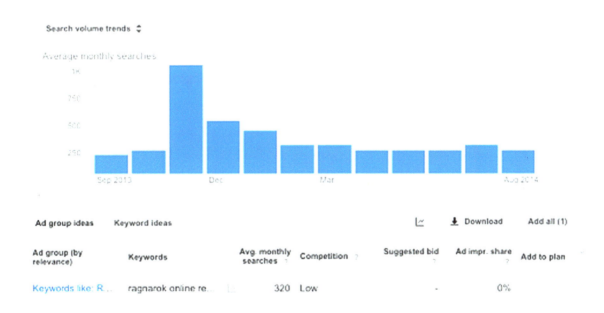

The AdWords Keyword Planner Tool tells you how many people are searching for that keyword every month.

When we look up the keywords *"Ragnarok Online review"* on **AdWords Keyword Planner** (the tool Google provides to see how often people make searches for different types of things) we can see that the numbers vary. During some months there are hundreds of searches for that topic, but during another month (November 2013) there were over 1,000 searches. By having my video at the #1 spot for the search results, it allowed my video to become discovered by people searching for the information in my video — which means it got more views than it would have if it had not been in the top spot.

If you do not take the time to find and include the right keywords for your video, you will only get views from people whom you directly share the video with. This takes a huge amount of time, and is not as ideal as optimizing your video for search queries; you want to put the search engines to work for you to help you get traffic.

To find out which kind of keywords will work well for your type of content, you should first exploit the market trends by searching for phrases that you think would be popular and related to your video. Then look at the data provided by the AdWords Keyword Planner to find a search phrase that has a high volume of searches every month. If you need some help, use the tool *http://keywordtool.io/* ; this site will tell you what popular search queries are being made around a subject. You can then take these terms and enter them into the AdWords Keyword Tool to find the search volume for these phrases so you can know how much traffic is possible if you rank your videos for this keywords.

What you want to do is look at the search volume (how many people will search for it within a month). Make sure that the keywords have a minimum of 300 searches in a single month. If it is less than 300 queries, it's not worth investing the time to SEO your video for the top spot of that search phrase.

What to Do with the Keywords

Once you have identified keywords, you need to include them in your video in such a way that YouTube will pull the meta-data and place your video into the top spots for search results.

This is done by properly filling out the video's fields for Title, Video Description and Tags.

Basic Info   Monetization   Advanced settings

The RPG Fanatic Review Show - ★Ragnarok Online Renewal Update

Public

Add a message to your video

Also share on

☑ G+ ☑ 🐦

📹 3 playlists

Ragnarok Online (Korean: 라그나로크 온라인, alternatively subtitled The Final Destiny of the Gods), often referred to as RO is a Korean massive multiplayer online role-playing game or MMORPG created by GRAVITY Co., Ltd. based on the manhwa Ragnarok by Lee Myung-jin. It was first released in South Korea on 31 August 2002 for Microsoft Windows and has since been released in many other locales around the world. The game has spawned an animated series, Ragnarok the Animation, and a sequel game, Ragnarok Online 2: Legend of the Second.

Review for the MMORPG Ragnarok Online by Gravity, Inc. If you decide to play the game, you might be interested in something I put together on my website, Ragnarok Online Renewal FAQ and Solo Leveling Guide
http://www.rpgfanatic.net/advanced_game_wiki_database.html?p=walkthroughs&wnd=5048&game=Ragnarok+Online

Player characters exist in a world with a player environment that gradually changes with the passage of time. Major changes in the features and history of the world take place as episodes in the RO timeline. Player characters interact in a 3D environment but are represented by 2D character sprites for front, back, side and diagonal facings. The major types of server-supported gameplay are Player vs Environment, Guild vs Guild, Player vs Player. Also supported by the game server are Group vs Group, Arena Combat, Player vs Monster, Player vs All, and various other specific scenarios at designated instance locations in the game world. NPC-run challenges and contests are also available with prizes, awards, and/or listing in a specific hall of fame listing.

Ragnarok Online is divided into a series of maps on two major continents, each of which has its own terrain and native monsters, though many monsters are present in multiple regions. Transportation between maps requires loading the new map and

1. Video Title should include ONE search phrase (the most popular)

2. The Video Description Field should have an article of 5,000 characters.

old games ×   games for 360 ×   latest new games ×

youtube rpg ×   rpg is ×   rpg video ×   video game ×

game nerd ×   video game nerds ×   video nerd ×

you tube movies for free ×   you tube plays ×   best video ×

online game rpg ×   download rpg games ×   pc rpg ×

online multiplayer games ×   school games ×   best games ×

best game ×   free games online ×   Gameplay ×

Mmorpg ×   Video Game ×   Computer ×   Review ×

Gamer ×   Reviews ×   ragnarok online 2 ×

ragnarok online ×   jobs ×   ragnarok 2 ×

ragnarok online gameplay ×   elsword ×

ragnarok gameplay ×

3. Tags field should have lots of search phrases.

You MUST completely fill out your Title, Video Description and Tags fields. Every possible character should be used; push it to the limits!

You should also upload a Closed Caption script to your video, as YouTube also uses the CC script to data-mine for keywords.

People usually go wrong by not including a 5,000 character article in the Video Description field.

Most YouTubers add a single sentence to their Video Description and then insert a bunch of links; **this is wrong.**

You **MUST** include an article of 5,000 characters into your Video Description fields, for **ALL** of your videos if you want to get search engine traffic. If you do not do this, you will **NOT** get much traffic to your videos from the search results. This is because YouTube and Google are search engines that use **TEXT** to determine what a video is about. You must provide enough **WORDS** for it to determine what keywords your video should rank for.

The audio in your video...the visuals in your video search engines can see none of it. All they can see about your video is the text in your Video's Title, Description, Tags and Closed Caption scripts. That's it.

If your video has a house exploding in it, search engines have no way of knowing that unless you literally write *"house exploding"* into your Video Description field. This is why it is so extremely important to fill out your video description fields properly.

Additionally, the CPM of your video will be based on the average bid price of the keywords your video is ranking for. I have seen a lot of creators who have managed to get hundreds of thousands of views to their channel every month, but they only make a few hundred dollars in ad revenue. They could have been making over $10,000 if they had simply included a 5,000 character article into their video description that had keywords with a high bid price on AdWords.

It is very easy to make a 5,000 character article for your videos; Wikipedia provides tons of articles that can be used under their Creative Commons license. You can use sections of a Wikipedia article as a starting point for your Video Description article, and simply insert the high search volume keyword phrases that you found from AdWords Keyword Planner into the article.

Try Making Videos Based on Popular Searches

For best results, try to first identify keywords that receive hundreds of thousands of queries a month before actually creating your video. Also. write the script for your video in such a way that it will meet the needs of the people making the search for that topic.

Building videos based on what people are searching for may not sound as fun as making videos about whatever you want to make them about, but it is a better formula for success. You can be sure that there are people who are interested in watching the video that is about a popular search phrase.

I encourage you to play around with the AdWords Keyword tools to create a great and original video for YouTube fans to enjoy.

Advanced Video Settings

Fill in everything as much as possible. Set Caption Certificate to *"This has never been aired..."* and click the 'Today' option for your recording date.

Again, YouTube uses all of this meta-data to help your video appear in search results and Related video feeds. Other apps that use YouTube also use the location field.

Fill everything out!

Setup Your Playlists

You'll want to create Playlists of curated videos and add them to your channel page to make your videos easier to find.

Section 2. Setting up Annotations

"Curate your content". This means that you should use video annotations to alert someone watching one of your videos to other videos you have made. I actually made a video of my own detailing the process, which I created to show some friends how to do it.

Section 3. Adding a Closed Caption Script

Closed-captioning is a subtitling process intended to allow the deaf and hearing-impaired to enjoy videos without hearing them. YouTube supports closed-captioning, but it's valuable for reasons that are not obvious. The single greatest tip I could give anyone on how to improve their video's rank in YouTube Search results is to add a close captions script to all the videos they upload. This is because YouTube Search cannot detect what is in your audio files to find keywords to improve your search rankings. Instead, it looks at the text in your Title, Video Description, Tags and Closed Caption script.

YouTube does use a "machine" script deploying voice recognition technology in an effort to create a closed-caption script, but it often generates gibberish because any sound or music in the video will cause problems in the recognition process.

That being said, there is a little known-feature for uploading your own closed-caption script to your videos. YouTube uses the same recognition technology to match a pre-written script to timecodes in your video. Because you gave it a list to follow, it is able to be 99% accurate with its time-code matching to the dialogue in your video.

What this means is that if you write a text file (.txt; you can make it in Notepad or Microsoft Office) with everything that you say in your video and upload it to your video, YouTube will be able to use your text file to generate a closed caption script for you.

This is such an easy thing to do that there is no reason to not do it. Better yet, every word and phrase in your script is going to be considered a keyword, helping your video gain more visibility in YouTube Search results.

Section 4. Understanding the Related Videos Feed

The Related Video Feed is a gallery of videos appearing at the right hand side of the YouTube video watch screen, and also appearing at the end of a video. The videos that are featured are determined by many factors, such as the keywords used in the videos, how popular the videos are and other such data. In a lot of cases, the Related Video Feed is just a "Walled Garden" of your own channel videos, and there are few spots to showcase from other creators.

Despite it being notoriously difficult to manipulate your videos into someone else's related video feed, many YouTubers will spend hours trying different keyword combinations in an attempt to have their videos featured in the Related Video Feed of popular YouTube videos.

Although it can be a great source of traffic, placing all your hopes and dreams on the Related Videos Feeds will probably end in disappointment.

When a video is heavily promoted by the Related Video Feeds on high traffic videos, it is largely due to sheer dumb luck. It is not something that you can control, and it has little to do with the quality of the video. High traffic videos are more likely to display other videos from the person who made the video than they are to show someone else's videos. This has been my experience with videogame related videos and I imagine it is the same for other kinds of content too.

The lesson to learn here is to **promote your videos OUTSIDE of YouTube!**

Section 5. InVideo Programming, FanFinder

YouTube Top Fan G+ Circles

This is a new feature (as of 2013) that allows you to create a Google+ Circle from your engaged subscribers if you have at least 1,000 subscribers to your channel.

If you have access to the feature, you can access it at *https://www.youtube.com/audience*

InVideo Programming

InVideo Programming is a way to place a video annotation on your videos to advertise them. You can use it for your own videos, or the videos of other YouTubers whom you are cross-promoting with.

You can access this tool at *https://www.youtube.com/account_featured_programming*

Fan Finder

The Fan Finder feature allows you to designate a video (ideally less than 90 seconds in length) as a free ad that YouTube will attempt to show to YouTubers who might be interested in your show. There is a credit system in place so that for every x number of organic views your YouTube channel receives, you earn 1 credit of Fan Finder promotion.

The precise ratio of organic videos : Fan Finder displays is not publicly known, but testing has shown that you need to have tens of thousands of views per month for Fan Finder to do anything for your channel.

You can access the Fan Finder tool for your channel at *https://www.youtube.com/fan_finder*

Please watch the following video tutorial for a more in-depth discussion about these features.

How to Prevent Trolling Attacks on Your YouTube Videos

Trolling from immature commentors has been a big source of frustration for many YouTubers. Some people often feel helpless about their ability to stop trolls from using multiple accounts to upvote nasty video comments, and then to make those comments the "Featured Comment."

These kind of attacks often hurt the feelings of the creator who has poured a lot of time and energy into producing their videos. It can discourage them when they constantly see the top rated comment for their video is a nasty troll remark.

Well good news YouTubers! Your account has some features to reduce the ability for a troll to launch these kinds of attacks.

Go to *https://www.youtube.com/comment_management* and you whill be presented with several fields that allow you to approve commentors, ban commentors and set parameters for the featured comment section of your videos.

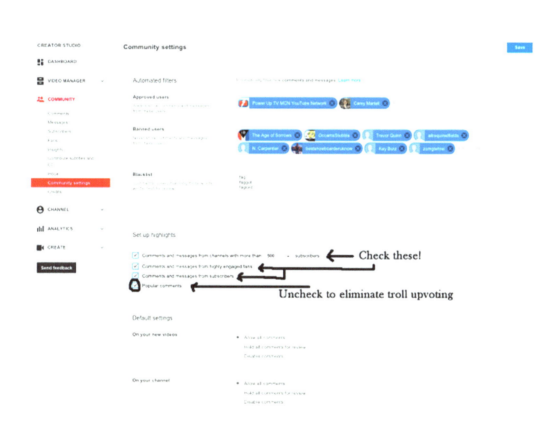

What you want to do is uncheck the "Popular comments" section under "Set up highlights," while also checking the boxes for the other parameters. This will make it so that the trolls who use multiple dummy accounts to upvote their own comments cannot get their comments featured anymore.

The "Featured comment" slot will instead go to fans who are engaged on all your videos and actively watch your show, or to channels that have large subscriber bases themselves.

Once you implement these changes, you will find that trolls are less inclined to spend time harassing your videos as their efforts have less impact.

As always, you should also not "feed the trolls"; that is, do not respond to their comments. Focus instead on responding to the people who post constructive comments on your videos, and engage with them. You need to **cultivate relationships with users** in order to build loyal subscribers.

Section 6. Cross-Promotion with Other YouTubers

Cross-Promote with Other Partners

The people who become the most successful on YouTube find their success because they are doing one of two things:

1. Tapping into audiences outside of YouTube, such as from Facebook Pages, mailing lists or notable websites with a lot of daily visitors.

-OR-

2. Someone with an already established YouTube audience is plugging them on their channel.
However, even with a plug from a YouTube superstar, you are not guaranteed to get that many views. For example, *my interview with egoraptor* was pimped on his YouTube channel feed, his Facebook Fan page and his Twitter, but it only gained 17,045 views. At the time, egoraptor had about five hundred thousand subscribers, and his videos get over a million views (each within a few days of uploading). So what is the problem? Why did my video that he pimped not get even a few hundred thousand views?

Well, I don't know for sure, but here is my best guess:

Back then I noticed egoraptor favorited a *JonTron* video......

...and JonTron had egoraptor in his recommended channel list.

I then noticed that Egoraptor also has JonTron in his recommended channel list.

I realized the top Partners who are consciously competent at using YouTube realize **networking with other Partners** is the best way to expand awareness of their videos. You cannot just upload videos into the vast sea of YouTube and hope that they float to the top of the charts. You have to **market them**. Networking with other partners who have audiences similar to the ones you want to attract can be a very effective way to expand.

Even though egoraptor had a lot of subscribers, only a fraction of them live and breath his channel; most are folks who hardly ever log in to their channels and thus do not see his subscription feed activity. To get millions of views, egoraptor needed a network of other YouTube stars to cross-promote his new videos, which allowed him to be seen by the die-hard fans of his friends.

Here is another thing to consider.

Let's say that I am a big YouTube Partner who makes videogame reviews, but only about roleplaying games *(not too much of a stretch, I guess?).*

The people who search for my content using YouTube's search bar, and who see my videos in Related Video Feeds are most likely doing a search relevant to the particular game that I uploaded a review for. For example, I might have a *review for Final Fantasy Mystic Quest* and people might come across my channel while doing a search for "Final Fantasy Mystic Quest." However, if they are searching for something like Minecraft or The Elder Scrolls: Skyrim, my videos will never come up because I have no reviews for those games.

That means that the overwhelming majority of people who search for videogame related content are **never** going to see my videos, because they aren't searching for the specific reviews that I've uploaded. Just because I put generic keywords like "rpgs" and "video game" into my description and tag area does not mean jack! That is not enough to make my videos appear in generic search results for "rpgs" or "videogames"-- not when millions of other videos are also using those same tags.

There are legions of people who would be interested in my videos, but only a fraction of them will find my videos by doing a search.

So what do you do if you want to tap into audiences on YouTube who might be interested in your content?

Networking 101

You have to network with someone who has a fanbase similar to the one you want or already have, and you share audiences by helping plug one another.

And not just once or twice, or merely sticking them into your "recommended channels" sidebar to gather dust. Every day, you must be liking, favoriting and commenting on their videos so that they get seen in the subscription feeds of users--- **and they must do the same thing for you!**

Many YouTube users are subscribed to hundreds of channels -- many of whom post several vblogs a day. There is *A LOT* of stuff that goes into your subscription feed that you never see unless you sit on Youtube all day long (and even then....but we'll get to that later).

You also need to expand your plugging efforts outside of Youtube. You have to promote one another on your Twitter and Facebook Fan pages too.

Here is one thing that some people get short-sighted about: You do not need to only network with big channels.

As an example, I used to have 2,793 subscribers on my *'jfreedan'* channel, and 1,639 on *TheRPGFanatic channel.* My friend *8-Bit Eric* had 2,513 on his channel. Eric and I both liked, favorited and commented on each other's channels, and over time we have both built up over 13,000 subscribers to our individual channels.

Now, I must point out that the number of subscribers are just the best possible number of eyeballs you can reach; it's the *potential views*.

Realistically each plug you do may only get 20%-40% of the potential views obtainable -- which is why you **continually** like, favorite and comment on each other's videos! Eventually you will find that a very high portion of the subscribers of one channel have gone and viewed the videos on everyone else's channel.

The more quality YouTube channels that you include in your cross-promotion super friends group, the more effective this strategy will be.

Web Rings

This is not a brand new tactic. Way back when the internet was young and "Bert Is Evil" memes were all the rage, we called this forming a 'web ring'. Everyone would embed links into our website leading to other websites who were part of the group, and we often had banner exchanges that rotated each members' banner every time someone loaded the page. Our news pages would have links to something that had been posted to another person's website. Webcomics still promote each other this way, and that is relevant because just like videos, a webcomic primarily consists of content that cannot be crawled by search engines.

The problem is this: when trying to network, you come across a lot of people who are not committed to the cause. They put you into their recommended channel space, do a little bit of promotion, and then forget to do it later on. Sometimes they even watch your videos and do not comment, favorite or like them, because "*I* *forgot".*

They have a million excuses for why they cannot keep the promotion up, ranging from, *"I don't want to upset my subscribers"* to *"I am too busy with school".*

Then there are the people who do not want to make a Facebook Fan page, **even though it's one of the MOST effective ways to ensure that your subscribers see your latest videos.**

If someone refuses to share your videos in return for you sharing theirs, stop sharing their videos. They are not fulfilling their end of the deal, so find other people to work with.

Networking with channels smaller than your own

Another thing to consider is that if you help build up someone who does not have a lot of subscribers, you are ultimately helping create a new audience for your own work.

Does that sound weird? Let me explain.

Let's suppose I have 500 of my subscribers become followers of someone else's channels- let's call him Bob. Of those 500, about 50 of them actually share all of Bob's videos on their Facebook pages. Of those 50 about 10 more people check out Bob's page and subscribe. A handful of them actually share some of Bob's videos on a big forum like The Escapist, bringing Bob several hundred more subscribers.

All these new subscribers from The Escapist who came to look at Bob's videos probably have never heard of my content before-- but they will when they see Bob share my latest video in his YouTube, Twitter and Facebook activity feeds.

There is actually a lot of benefit to people with larger fanbases to help small channels grow. A lot of people just get tunnel vision and want to take the quick and easy route of getting someone like egoraptor to pimp their stuff constantly.

Where to Find Collaborators

You can also look at subreddits like *http://www.reddit.com/r/YouTubeGamers/* that have threads for people to post collaboration requests.

You should also network at various real-world events, such as conventions like VidCon, Playlist Live and your local meetup groups.

If there are no local groups for YouTubers in your area, perhaps you should consider making one?

I founded the *Austin YouTube Partner meetup group* so that I could network with other YouTubers in Austin, Texas. I also attend many networking events for film-makers and video professionals.

Pro Tip: *Order up some business cards for yourself to hand out to anyone you'd like to work with. I have business cards that have my name, email address, YouTube channel and cell phone number so that it is very easy for people to contact me.*

If you are in the Los Angeles area, attending *YouTube Space LA* events is another great way to meet other creators that you can collaborate with. Every time that I go to Los Angeles, I try to attend the Happy Hour events and always meet a lot of creators.

LinkedIn

LinkedIn is a social network for professionals, and that includes entertainment folks working in the web video space.

If you do not have a LinkedIn account, *make one.* Every time you reveice a business card from a YouTuber, add that person's email address as a contact on your LinkedIn profile. This will allow you to reach other YouTubers they are connected to through LinkedIn, greatly expanding your professional rolodex of fellow creators who are also professional minded like you.

Quiz Questions: Collaborating with YouTubers

1. The most popular YouTubers grew their audiences all by themselves without working with anyone else. (True / False)

2. What kind of YouTuber should you collaborate with?
  A. Anyone who will work with me.
  B. Someone who has a totally different audience than me.
  C. Someone who has a similar type of audience as I do.

3. How many subscribers does another YouTuber need in order for it to be useful to cross-promote with them?
  A. Over one-million subscribers
  B. Over nine-thousand!!!!
  C. They need to have around the same number of subscribers as my own channel.
  C. The specific number of subscribers they have doesn't matter. They just need to have an audience that might also like my videos.

4. Every day I should be sharing, commenting and liking on the videos of other YouTubers I am cross-promoting with. (True / False)

5. I should continue to promote the videos of YouTubers who are not sharing my videos in return. (True / False)

6. I should try to meet other YouTube creators in person and ask them to collaborate with me. (True / False)

7. I should make a business card with my real name, phone number and email address on it. I should give this card to other YouTubers so they can contact me about collaborations and ideas they have in the future. (True / False)

Section 7. Facebook Pages for Beginners

Having a Facebook Fan Page is crucial to your success on YouTube, for several reasons.

Firstly, even if you only have a small number of fans liking your page, you can still have a lot of reach. For example, even when I only had 346 fans on *The RPG Fanatic Fan Page* I was able to reach 1,917 people with my status updates.

This is because as fans 'like' a post, they also share it with their friends in their status feeds, and they can 'share' your Fan Page posts on their wall. This allows you to embed a video into a status update of your Facebook Fan Page, and then have that video circulated throughout the social networks of Facebook.

I have Facebook Fan Pages for every project that I have created, ranging from books I've published to movies I've made. All of my websites have a Facebook Fan Page embedded into them.

Additionally, you can use your Fan page to create an event, such as announcing your next livestream or a convention panel that you plan on holding.

Facebook Page Promotion

Facebook Pages can be a powerful tool for growing your audience. The nice thing about Facebook Promoted Posts is that you can target specific demographics and even select people by what topics they are interested in.

If you have a lot of Facebook friends, it's not too hard to make a Page and get a following started. You can mass invite your friends using the "Build Audience" section of your Page.

1. Scheduling Posts

Managing a Facebook Page takes a lot of work. To keep people interested, you need to constantly supply them with new posts. Using the Page scheduling feature allows me to spend 15 minutes of my day scheduling content for the next few weeks; this ensures that the Page has a steady flow of content. I generally schedule content to be released twice a day; once at 3 PM CST and again at 6 PM CST. I also re-schedule old videos after having published them 2-3 weeks ago. Because I have a large library of videos, it is easy for me to keep the Page regularly populated.

Scheduled Posts

The RPG Fanatic

Does anyone remember Azure Dreams? It was one of my favorite games when it first came out. http://www.youtube.com/watch?v=H1g_p2I5S-Y

The RPG Fanatic Review Show – ★ Azure Dreams Review ★
www.youtube.com
Review for Azure Dreams (PS1) by Konami (1998). Azure Dreams, released in Japan as Other Life: Azure Dreams (アナザー・ライフ・アゼル・ドリームズ）

The RPG Fanatic

Do you like epic boss battles? Here's some clips of my character battling a zombie dragon in Dragon's Dogma: Dark Arisen. https://www.youtube.com/watch?v=4mjVkUMn0C8

Epic Boss Battle – Dragon's Dogma: Cursed Dragon
www.youtube.com
Cursed dragons fight with a combination of Ur-Dragon like moves and some original ones. The only difference is the smaller size of Cursed Dragons, and instea...

The RPG Fanatic

Have you ever seen such a crazy controller before? I think it was forged in the pits of the netherworld for the Dark Prince himself. https://www.youtube.com/watch?v=7aHYwre4Sj4

What the Hell Is This?! – The Devil Head Video Game PS1 Controller
www.youtube.com
https://www.facebook.com/TheRPGFanatic Seriously, what the hell is this thing? I've been totally unable to figure out where it comes...

The RPG Fanatic

This question is still relevant. Do you want a comprehensive review of the entire SaGa series? https://www.youtube.com/watch?v=g3AdvXJFPyg

Should I do a Retrospective Video on the SaGa series?
www.youtube.com
https://www.facebook.com/TheRPGFanatic I have a question for my fans. Should I do an in-depth review of all the SaGa series games or should I just review Rom...

Show More

2. Buying Promoted Posts

After my posts are released to the Page, I purchase a promotion campaign for the posts to get them seen by people who live in the United States **AND** have specifically said that they like the game I am reviewing. When done correctly with a good call to action, you can get a lot of engagement to grow your audience.

As an example, I did a review for *Castlevania: Symphony of the Night* and then created this Facebook post to promote it.

Another example is my *SaGa Frontier* review,

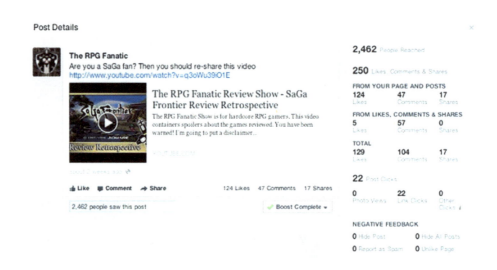

In both cases I targeted individuals who said that they liked the game titles I reviewed. The ad was not shown to anyone else but the people most likely to engage with the content. This is the correct way to use Promoted Posts on Facebook.

After someone has liked your post, if you click on the "...people liked this" link at the bottom of your post you, will be presented with a menu allowing you to invite these people to follow your Page. In this way you can very effectively grow an audience on Facebook.

Facebook Power Editor

If you have a mailing list, you can use the **Facebook Power Editor's** Audiences tab to target specific Facebook users with laser accuracy. You can make sure that your ads only get seen by the people who are members of your mailing list; Facebook will match their email addresses to their Facebook accounts to allow you to target them.

You can also build lists of "similar users" to those who have already liked your Facebook Page.

Section 8. Twitter for Beginners

Twitter is a popular service but in my opinion it is a bit tougher to use for marketing compared to Facebook. This is because the majority of the users send tweets, but don't necessarily read tweets.

Still, you might be able to nab some new subscribers to your channel if you use it appropriately.

Websites like Twitter -- social networks -- are very powerful tool for marketing and promoting. If you want to quickly spread the news about your newest activities or businesses, then the best solution for you is to have an account on well-known socialization sites like Twitter and Facebook.

Thousands of people join Twitter every day, or share opinions and other information with the help of Twitter; why shouldn't you use its powers in your YouTube marketing strategy? Do so and you will soon notice that word about you spreads faster than you think. Before you get there though, there are some things that you need to take care off first.

Setting up Your Profile

*My **personal Twitter profile** is complete, having a custom banner, profile picture, links and a description. You need to have an interesting and complete profile on Twitter.*

Put some effort when you are building it; if people consider the content interesting, it will be much easier to engage them and even convince them to follow you. This is why you should choose a real picture of you. Even if you promote a business, people like to get in touch with other people and feel like there is an actual person at the other end of the computer screen.

You should also give your location; people like to know where you are from, and often search for creators in their local area.

Make sure that the information you put on your profile is interesting and covers all areas of interest. If you want to promote something, list the most intriguing aspects of your activity or business.

Also, add a link to your YouTube channel / personal website so that people who discover you on Twitter can easily find your show.

Who to Follow?

People that you might come into contact with may find interesting information that they want to share with you, or they may be celebrities/public people that you admire for their work. You can choose to follow them on Twitter by clicking on the *"follow"* button; this makes your tweet always appear on your tweet list. It also enables everyone in your friend list to see who are you following, and thus this circle may increase.

You can also find people talking about certain topics on Twitter, by simply **searching the topic word you are interested in.** When you find an interesting discussion on your favorite topic, you can choose to follow that person. As a result, information connects from one user to another. Finding friends and people that you may know can occur the same manner; just type a name and you will see a list of persons from where to choose.

I recommend that you follow as many people as possible. Twitter has an established culture of people reciprocating follows, so by following many people you can get many follows in return.

Another way to get your information organized on Twitter is by using hashtags (#). If you are new to Twitter this may seem an odd term for you. Just pay a little attention and follow the explanations that are about to come.

Anyone can do a hashtag at any time, and in any conversation just by adding the symbol "#" to any words. Do not include any space between the # sign and the word (just like *"#YouTube")*. This should mark keywords in your conversation and by adding this mark to your keyword, anyone will be able to find your tweets (and others) that discuss this topic.

An example of a YouTube video I tweeted with some trending hashtags, #DargonQuest and #DargonQuestMyGame.

If your hashtag is the only one on a certain topic, only your tweet will appear in the list when other people use the search function. For this reason, it makes sense to choose hashtags that other people already are using.

You can research trending hashtags at various third-party websites, such as...
* **http://trendsmap.com/**
* **http://www.whatthetrend.com/**
* **http://www.hashtags.org/trending-on-twitter/**

Using hashtags will definitely make it easier for you to get in touch with people; it expands the number of people who can see your tweets beyond your personal subscribers.

Twitter Etiquette

Twitter has some etiquette regarding hashtags. It is recommend that you should use a maximum of two hashtags in a single tweet, so choose only the words that are most relevant to your topic. By using hashtags, it becomes easier for people to find you and the information that you are promoting.

You should also follow back anyone that follows you, and the same goes for those who retweet (share) and favorite your tweets.

This "you follow me, I follow you" behavior can actually be exploited in order to grow your Twitter profile audience. Many successful YouTubers utilize tools to first scrape the followers of another YouTuber who produces similar content, and then to follow the profiles of each user in the list. This allows you to introduce your content (by way of your Twitter profile posts) to people who are most likely to be interested in it.

To assist with this strategy you can purchase third party software like TweetNuke.

How to Get Video Traffic from StumbleUpon

Having a YouTube channel is nothing much if you do not have the proper traffic for it. You probably did not create your videos just for you to watch.

In order to get views to your video channel, you need to do everything in your power to bring traffic to your videos if you want to be successful and turn your web series into a hit.

Luckily there are some ways — more specifically, some tools — you can use to get significant increases in traffic. One of the most effective among these tools is StumbleUpon. To get an idea about how good this website is, you should know that in the beginning of the year 2011, StumbleUpon exceeded Facebook in bringing traffic to websites. This is why you should also use it to increase the chances of your web series becoming discovered.

Here is what you need to know when using StumbleUpon to get traffic increase.

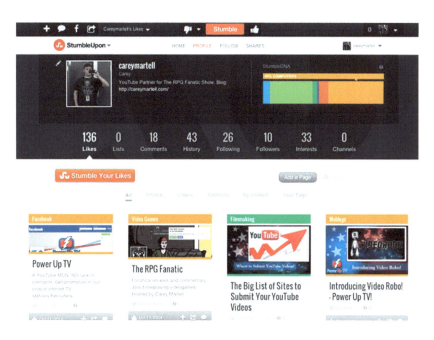

Make sure your profile is completed.

When using such a powerful tool, you should put some time and effort into creating a proper profile. Add a good picture and make sure that the information you upload is real and complete. Make a list of your interests, so that it will be easier for other users to tell if you are a person interesting enough for them to make connections with. Do not try to trick the system by creating more than one account. It will not bring you more traffic; you will simply be banned from the site.

If you'd like an example of a profile, you can check out my personal one at **http://www.stumbleupon.com/ stumbler/careymartell**

For a better use of your time on this site, you should *install the browser toolbar specially designed for StumbleUpon.* By doing this, sharing content will be only a click away. It will also help mark your own website or new blog posts, so that people can stumble onto them easier.

Develop a good strategy for content placement.

Use the opportunity of being a StumbleUpon member wisely, and be careful about the content that you are putting here. Avoid marketing yourself too much, because people are not here to only see news about you. If all of your posts are only from your own YouTube channel, you are likely to get your account flagged as a spammer.

As with everything on the Internet today, having good quality content is very important here. Posting videos that other users enjoy will help you develop a good reputation, and will also make people want to search through all of the submissions your profile has made. In addition, make sure that some of the submissions you make are from your personal website.

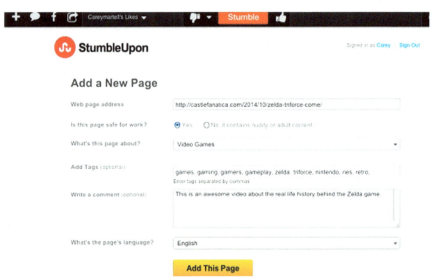

When submitting a new page, be sure to completely fill out the profile, including selecting multiple keyword tags related to the video.

When making submissions from your YouTube videos, make sure your video has an original title and a custom thumbnail, as these two items will be seen in the submission listings that you create. If the title and thumbnail are both very interesting, people will click on your submission instead of others. If you teach people that you are the one that will always have interesting things to share, then they will come searching for you and your channel. You have already created an image of yourself as being an interesting person that has great things to offer.

Establish connections with other members too.

StumbleUpon is a social site, and you should treat it accordingly. It was created for people to find information that is usually very hard to discover because it does not rank at the top of search engine results.

Depending on a user's profile settings, you may be able to send them a personal message.

If you want to increase your traffic and bring success to your website, then the community you find here might help you do that. Thus, connect with people that share the same interests as yourself and your channel's content. You should check out the profiles of members to see if you have anything in common with them.

Be personal when sharing content with the other members, and do not forget to pass on the shares you also receive. This is a two way relationship, if you mean it to be fruitful.

If you follow these tips, you should get some positive organic results from StumbleUpon.

Section 9. Analyzing the data

This is where most creators go wrong. They forget that YouTube is a sophisticated piece of technology that uses complex mathematical algorithms to determine what videos appear in search result pages and related video feeds. You must give the platform enough data to know where to place your video, or it will not be able to do its job.

There are many tools on the market to pull data from, but we at Thunder TV developed Video Robo to get a general sense of how different channels are doing.

I also created an account at *VideoLC,* which is a service that looks at my channel's data to tell me a few things. It will generate a report manually, or email me one every Monday about a few topics:

- The best days and times to release new videos

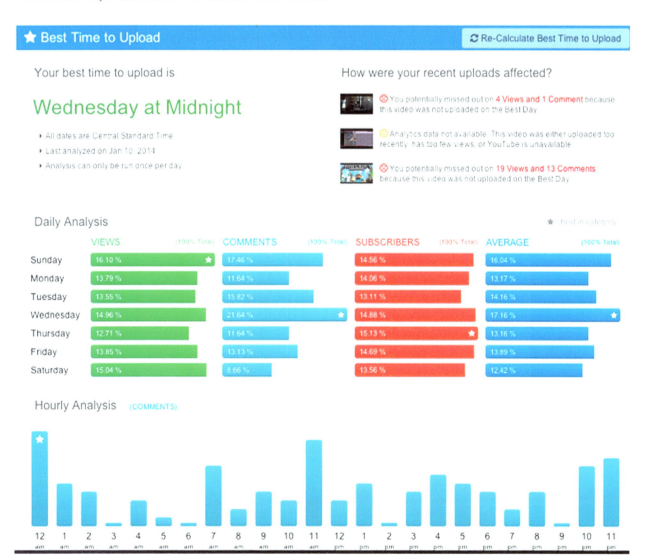

- How well my videos rank for high search volume keywords, and how to improve the rankings

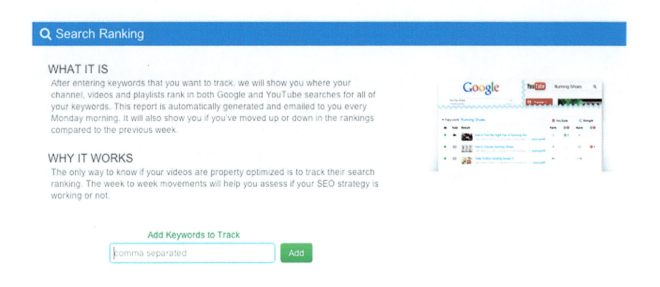

VideoLC tells me the most often used keywords in video descriptions, and also tags that appear on the front page of results. This helps me improve my own video's ranking.

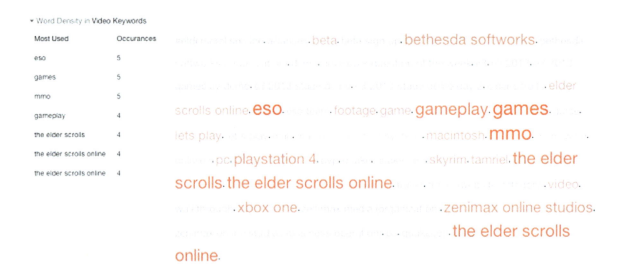

- Results of A/B (split-marketing) video thumbnail tests

- Detailed analysis of how many views my channel receives per day, (which helps me know how many videos I need in my back library in order to reach millions of videos per day)

VideoLC software is really good stuff, and I highly recommend it.

Other Pointers

1.	**Use YouTube's built-in tools.** The new *Fan Insight tool* can help you make a G+ Circle of your fans, and regularly try to engage with them. Also make sure you upload a closed-caption transcript (just make a .txt file with everything you said; YouTube will associate the words with your video automatically). In addition, set the GPS location of your video, and set a create date; these features are more relevant for things like Google Maps and third-party apps. Every little bit helps.

2.	**Make an email list.** I suggest using FanBridge and asking your subscribers to join it so that you can send them regular updates. Offer perks only available to email subscribers like unlisted video blogs or gift cards contests.

3.	**Setup a *Google Alert* for your channel name.** This will let you know where people are talking about you, so that you can better engage with the communities that are watching your content.

4.	**Make a *thunderclap.it*.** Thunderclap is kind of like a Groupon for mass social sharing. After a specific number of people agree to share a topic on sites like Facebook or Twitter, Thunderclap will auto-share the message to their walls at all once. This can help build a trending topic. I have not used this personally for my channel (yet), but I have used it for other things quite successfully. It is meant for sharing causes and events, so use it responsibly. Create some kind of event related to your channel, or tie your video to an event, and you should have no problems.

5.	**Engage with users who comment.** This should go without saying but YouTube is a social network. You need to talk to people who are commenting on your videos, because that is what they are doing - talking to you. This an opportunity to build a community around your channel (a tribe of fellow gamers, if you will). Another thing that I did when reviving my channel was to look at how many people had commented on videos, compared with how many had subscribed. There was a huge number of comments that did not result in subscriptions. I formed them into a list and then reached out to them, encouraging them to see my latest video and subscribe to be notified of new ones.

Section 10. Building a Social Following

"If you build it they will come" is a lovely sentiment, but not realistic. The fact of the matter is you must take action to make folks aware of your community in order to grow it.

There are two basic components needed to build an online community, especially one based around a YouTube channel:

1. People

2. Valuable Content

To explain what is meant by *People* and *Valuable Content*, we will discuss each one separately.

People

There are two specific types of people that you need to build an online community:

1. Your Customers (i.e. your audience)

2. Influencers (the leaders, innovators, and voices particular to your industry)

The bulk of your community members will generally be silent; you will see their views add to your YouTube Analytics meters, but they will never comment on your videos. They are passive-consumers.

By contrast, the influencers are active-consumers; they will not only comment on your videos, but also talk about the video elsewhere such as their Facebook wall or their personal blogs. They will re-share your content more often (and regularly) than anyone else will.

Have you ever seen a YouTube video that has millions of views, but only several thousand 'likes' and re-shares? This is because influencers make up a smaller portion of a community; they are the ones who are willing to engage with content. They are a smaller group, but they are the main reason why content can "go viral", because they are the ones who share content with their own communities.

The take away from this is that if you focus your community building on having a relationship with influencers, you will get more customers.

Yes, a relationship. Community building is really about *relationships*.

Relationships are created by:

- Listening and responding
- Caring and taking the time to understand
- Providing valuable advice or insight

You must find the balance between entertainment and profundity in order to build a successful community.

Content

You cannot build an online community without people, and you cannot get people unless you have good content. Let us define content: it is not just videos. Content is ALL information (whether visual, audial, or audiovisual) that is built around your brand and designed to be consumed by your customers (i.e. your audience).

This means Content is...

- Videos uploaded to your YouTube channel
- Blog articles on your website
- Social media profile messages (tweets and posts)
- Podcasts
- Printed materials, such as flyers you hand out at events
- White papers
- Infographics
- DVDs / Blu-Rays
- Books
- Songs downloads

When I talk about content in this article and elsewhere, I am always referring to all of the above things. Do not just focus on videos; you must to consider everything that you create around your brand to be content.

It is very challenging these days to build a new community from scratch. There are millions of websites providing content, and many of them are run by experts who specialize in all kinds of niche subjects.

Simply having good content is no longer enough. You need to produce something wholly original in order to get a large number of followers. This is essential not only for YouTube-based businesses, but also for any type of business.

Nowadays it is extremely hard to find a subject that has not been discussed in depth, so the best way to stand out from the crowd is to focus on developing a creative way to show the same information (a unique presentation that will be attractive to a wide audience). This means that you should focus on producing quality rather than quantity.

The two types of content people most like to share is *stuff that is funny or motivational.*

If your videos do not fit into either category, your Facebook content should conform to one of these models, or people are not going to re-share it to their communities.

It is important to have a collection of memes, either *funny things of interest to your followers or motivational statements of interest to your followers.*

The important part here is *"..of interest to your followers."*

If you have a Facebook Page about videogames, do not post funny animal images onto the wall. Keep the content focused around the topic of videogames.

An Important Note

A Community Manager is not just another PR employee at your company who moderates your forums and social profiles. A Community Manager must be someone that is truly part of the community. This individual is someone who knows your brand and how to relate it to the community in order to continue building that community.

Promoting Your Content

For Twitter, you can buy promoted tweets to kick-start some growth to your account. On Facebook, you can also buy promoted posts. I encourage you to do both, as this will guarantee that people see your posts.

Of course there are free ways to get your content seen as well, such as re-sharing the content on your own accounts, but these efforts will rarely get you as many views as paid posts will. That being said, over time as you acquire more influencers in your community you will see more organic sharing of your content.

You should focus on generating two important types of content; these two types have the largest influence over the formation and growth of a community.

•   **Foundational** type of content is the solid base of your channel. You can consider this content to be the walls that sustain the entire business. These are the videos that best represent what your channel is about. These type of videos have a consistent formula that changes very little over time. This content should offer the best value for your audience, and constitute the main portion of your content production.

•   **Community-generated** type of content is the content that your community members create as a response to your Foundational content. This is everything from fan-fiction, to fan-art, to posts that they make in your community forums. The Community-generated content is the most dynamic part of your brand. It is often unpredictable, but this is the content that best represents your brand values because it is based on your community's response to your brand. This content is not created to advance your brand, but rather it is created by your community members in order for them to obtain a deeper sense of intimacy with your brand.

Before you see Community-generated content appear, you must first produce high value Foundational content. Usually you need to produce a lot of it. It may take months, or even years, for you to produce enough high value Foundational content before the brand becomes endearing enough to your community that they engage by producing Community-generated content.

A smartly developed strategy is all you need

Building an online community is all about Tactics. You cannot launch yourself into this matter without a well-developed plan. Otherwise you are producing content without any idea how your community is supposed to respond to it.

When developing your content production and release plan, you need to base the plan on two factors:

1. Consistency

2. Sustainability

Consistency means the content shares your brand image and has a consistent format. This means videos that use the same intro, have the same run-time, share the same host and talk about the same subjects. Consistency also means the content is released on a regular schedule.

Sustainability means that you can easily reproduce the formant of the content day after day, for months or years on end.

The most popular YouTubers do not produce million dollar TV episodes, but rather they produce 5 to 10 minute videos with little visual effects. At the most they may use a greenscreen, but often they only use transitions and motion graphics. They create a format where they can make 10-20 of these segments per day.

If you want to produce high-end TV show quality videos for your YouTube channel, you cannot build a single channel around this content because the high quality of the production values is not Sustainable. It is expensive and time-consuming to make these type of videos. The only way that producing these kind of videos can work is when that content is part of a YouTube channel that has a second show which has the ability to be both Consistent and Sustainable. The Sustainable show is the headliner of your channel, with the higher production quality show a second runner.

Last but Not Least

There is not just one recipe that will ensure success in building a community around your business. If your current strategy is not working as well as you had hoped, you just need to develop a newer, sturdier and more well-rounded strategy that will help you achieve the goals you want.

Also, always respect the content produced by your community, because good quality content will help increase the value of your brand and of your company. Respect your own brand values and goals, but also be sensitive to the informational flux. Take into consideration the comment posts you receive to your videos or blog, as this is feedback you are receiving.

This feedback can help you focus on customer needs and desires, while also helping you improve the quality of your content. Try to be flexible about this feedback; if things are not heading in the right direction you must be prepared for a change of plan, and possibly even a change in the format of your content.

Lastly, no matter what you produce, always make sure that both your brand goals and customer intentions are aligned.

FINAL THOUGHTS

Writing this book was a labor of love. Since 2005 I have dedicated my professional career to the business of video content production for internet distribution and used these lessons to grow two YouTube channel networks. Although the industry will continue to evolve rapidly as new technologies cause creators to constantly adapt their techniques and strategies, the core business principles will remain the same.

It is my hope this book will serve as a guide for many new entrepeneurs in the video entertainment space for years to come.

At my personal blog, CareyMartell.com , you will be able to find additional information about the space. If you found the information in this book useful i encourage you to check out my blog.

Good luck with your entrepeneurial journey!

Carey Martell
CEO, Martell Broadcasting Systems, Inc.

www.ingramcontent.com/pod-product-compliance
Lightning Source LLC
Chambersburg PA
CBHW050936060326
40689CB00040B/593